teacher friend publications

July & Aug.

a creative idea book
for the
elementary teacher

written and illustrated
by
Karen Sevaly

Copyright © Teacher's Friend,
a Scholastic Company
All rights reserved.
Printed in the U.S.A.

ISBN-13 978-0-439-50376-1
ISBN-10 0-439-50376-0

This book is dedicated
to teachers and children
everywhere.

Table of Contents

Making the most of it!

TF0700 July & August Idea Book

WHAT IS IN THIS BOOK:

You will find the following in each monthly idea book from Teacher's Friend Publications:

1. A calendar listing every day of the month with a classroom idea and mention of special holidays and events.

2. At least four student awards to be sent home to parents.

3. Three or more bookmarks that can be used in your school library or given to students by you as "Super Student Awards."

4. Numerous bulletin board ideas and patterns pertaining to the particular month and seasonal activity.

5. Easy-to-make craft ideas related to the monthly holidays and special days.

6. Dozens of activities emphasizing not only the obvious holidays, but also the often forgotten celebrations such as the first landing on the moon and the introduction of the ice cream cone.

7. Creative writing pages, crossword puzzles, word finds, booklet covers, games, paper bag puppets, literature lists and much more!

8. Scores of classroom management techniques and methods proven to motivate your students to improve behavior and classroom work.

HOW TO USE THIS BOOK:

Every page of this book may be duplicated for individual class-room use.

Some pages are meant to be copied or used as duplicating masters. Other pages may be transferred onto construction paper or used as they are.

If you have access to a print shop, you will find that many pages work well when printed on index paper. This type of paper takes crayons and felt markers well and is sturdy enough to last. (Bookmarks work particularly well on index paper.)

Lastly, some pages are meant to be enlarged with an overhead or opaque projector. When we say enlarge, we mean it! Think BIG! Three, four or even five feet is great! Try using colored butcher paper or poster board so you don't spend all your time coloring.

MONTHLY ORGANIZERS:

Staying organized month after month, year after year can be a real challenge. Try this simple idea:

After using the loose pages from this book, file them in their own file folder labeled with the month's name. This will also provide a place to save pages from other reproducible books along with craft ideas, recipes and articles you find in magazines and periodicals. (*Essential Pocket Folders* by Teacher's Friend provide a perfect way to store your monthly ideas and reproducibles. Each *Monthly Essential Pocket Folder* comes with a sixteen-page booklet of essential patterns and organizational ideas. There are even special folders for *Back to School*, *The Substitute Teacher* and *Parent-Teacher Conferences*.)

You might also like to dedicate a file box for every month of the school year. A covered box will provide room to store large patterns, sample art projects, certificates and awards, monthly stickers, monthly idea books and much more.

BULLETIN BOARD IDEAS:

Creating clever bulletin boards for your classroom need not take fantastic amounts of time and money. With a little preparation and know-how, you can have different boards each month with very little effort. Try some of these ideas:

1. Background paper should be put up only once a year. Choose colors that can go with many themes and holidays. The black butcher paper background you used as a spooky display in October will have a special dramatic effect in April with student-made, paper-cut butterflies.

2. Butcher paper is not the only thing that can be used to cover the back of your board. You might also try fabric from a colorful bed sheet or gingham material. Just fold it up at the end of the year to reuse again. Wallpaper is another great background cover. Discontinued rolls can be purchased for a small amount at discount hardware stores. Most can be wiped clean and will not fade like construction paper. (Do not glue wallpaper directly to the board; just staple or pin in place.)

3. Store your bulletin board pieces in large, flat envelopes made from two large sheets of tagboard or cardboard. Simply staple three sides together and slip the pieces inside. (Small pieces can be stored in zip-lock, plastic bags.) Label your large envelopes with the name of the bulletin board and the month and year you displayed it. Take a picture of each bulletin board display. Staple the picture to your storage envelope. Next year when you want to create the same display, you will know right where everything goes. Kids can even follow your directions when you give them a picture to look at.

ADDING THE COLOR:

Putting the color to finished items can be a real bother to teachers in a rush. Try these ideas:

1. On small areas, watercolor markers work great. If your area is rather large, switch to crayons or even colored chalk or pastels.

   (Don't worry, lamination or a spray fixative will keep color on the work and off of you. No laminator or fixative? That's okay, a little hair spray will do the trick.)

2. The quickest method of coloring large items is to start with colored paper. (Poster board, butcher paper or large construction paper work well.) Add a few dashes of a contrasting colored marker or crayon and you will have it made.

3. Try cutting character eyes, teeth, etc. from white typing paper and gluing them in place. These features will really stand out and make your bulletin boards come alive.

   For special effects, add real buttons or lace. Metallic paper looks great on stars and belt buckles, too.

LAMINATION:

If you have access to a roll laminator, then you already know how fortunate you are. They are priceless when it comes to saving time and money. Try these ideas:

1. You can laminate more than just classroom posters and construction paper. Try various kinds of fabric, wallpaper and gift wrapping. You'll be surprised at the great combinations you come up with.

   Laminated classified ads can be used to cut headings for current events bulletin boards. Colorful gingham fabric makes terrific cut letters or bulletin board trim. You might even try burlap! Bright foil gift wrapping paper will add a festive feeling to any bulletin board.

   (You can even make professional looking bookmarks with laminated fabric or burlap. They are great holiday gift ideas for Mom or Dad!)

2. Felt markers and laminated paper or fabric can work as a team. Just make sure the markers you use are permanent and not water-based. Oops, make a mistake! That's okay. Put a little ditto fluid on a tissue, rub across the mark and presto, it's gone! Also, dry transfer markers work great on lamination and can easily be wiped off.

LAMINATION:
(continued)

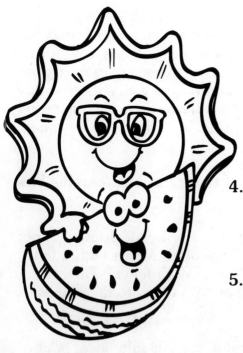

3. Laminating cut-out characters can be tricky. If you have enlarged an illustration onto poster board, simply laminate first and then cut it out with scissors or an art knife. (Just make sure the laminator is hot enough to create a good seal.)

One problem may arise when you paste an illustration onto poster board and laminate the finished product. If your paste-up is not 100% complete, your illustration and posterboard may separate after laminating. To avoid this problem, paste your illustration onto poster board that measures slightly larger than the illustration. This way, the lamination will help hold down your paste-up.

4. When pasting up your illustration, always try to use either rubber cement, artist's spray adhesive or a glue stick. White glue, tape or paste does not laminate well because it can often be seen under your artwork.

5. Have you ever laminated student-made place mats, crayon shavings, tissue paper collages, or dried flowers? You'll be amazed at the variety of creative things that can be laminated and used in the classroom or as take-home gifts.

PHOTOCOPIES AND DITTO MASTERS:

Many of the pages in this book can be copied for use in the classroom. Try some of these ideas for best results:

1. If the print from the back side of your original comes through the front when making a photocopy or ditto master, slip a sheet of black construction paper behind the sheet. This will mask the unwanted shadows and create a much better copy.

2. Several potential masters in this book contain instructions for the teacher. Simply cover the type with correction fluid or a small slip of paper before duplicating.

3. When using a new ditto master, turn down the pressure on the duplicating machine. As the copies become light, increase the pressure. This will get longer wear out of both the master and the machine.

4. Trying to squeeze one more run out of that worn ditto master can be frustrating. Try lightly spraying the inked side of the master with hair spray. For some reason, this helps the master put out those few extra copies.

LETTERING AND HEADINGS:

Not every school has a letter machine that produces perfect 4" letters. The rest of us will just have to use the old stencil-and-scissor method. But wait, there is an easier way!

1. Don't cut individual letters as they are difficult to pin up straight, anyway. Instead, hand print bulletin board titles and headings onto strips of colored paper. When it is time for the board to come down, simply roll it up to use again next year. If you buy your own pre-cut lettering, save yourself some time and hassle by pasting the desired statements onto long strips of colored paper. Laminate if possible. These can be rolled up and stored the same way!

   Use your imagination! Try cloud shapes and cartoon bubbles. They will all look great.

2. Hand lettering is not that difficult, even if your printing is not up to penmanship standards. Print block letters with a felt marker. Draw big dots at the end of each letter. This will hide any mistakes and add a charming touch to the overall effect.

   If you are still afraid to freehand it, try this nifty idea: Cut a strip of poster board about 28" X 6". Down the center of the strip, cut a window with an art knife measuring 20" X 2". There you have it: a perfect stencil for any lettering job. All you need to do is write capital letters with a felt marker within the window slot. Don't worry about uniformity. Just fill up the entire window height with your letters. Move your poster-board strip along as you go. The letters will always remain straight and even because the poster board window is straight.

3. If you must cut individual letters, use construction paper squares measuring 4 1/2" X 6". (Laminate first if you can.) Cut the capital letters as shown. No need to measure; irregular letters will look creative and not messy.

Calendar July & August

1ST   Today is CANADA DAY! The British established the Dominion of Canada on this day in 1867. (Display the Canadian flag in your classroom in celebration.)

2ND   THURGOOD MARSHALL, the first black U.S. Supreme Court Justice, was born on this day in 1908. It is also the anniversary of the CIVIL RIGHTS ACT of 1964. (Discuss with your class the changes that have taken place in racial equality.)

3RD   The Seminole Indians celebrate their new corn crop today with a GREEN CORN DANCE. (Ask your students to find out more about the celebration and where it takes place.)

4TH   Today is DECLARATION OF INDEPENDENCE DAY in the United States. (Celebrate by attending a community parade or having a family picnic.)

5TH   P.T. BARNUM, American circus showman, was born on this day in 1810. (Ask your students to discuss their favorite circus performers and acts.)

6TH   American naval hero JOHN PAUL JONES was born on this day in 1747. (Have your students research this interesting hero of the American Revolution.)

7TH   SATCHEL PAIGE, famous baseball player, was born on this day in 1839. (Ask your baseball fans to find out which position he played.)

8TH   American industrialist JOHN D. ROCKEFELLER was born on this day in 1839. (Ask your students to find out what contributions he made toward the building of our nation.)

9TH   ELIAS HOWE, inventor of the sewing machine, was born on this day in 1819. (Teach your students to use a sewing machine this summer. A simple craft, such as a pot holder, will be a great gift for Mom this holiday season.)

10TH   American artist JAMES McNEILL WHISTLER was born on this day in 1834. (Ask your students to find a picture of his most well-known painting.)

11TH   American children's author E.B. WHITE was born on this day in 1899. (This is a good time to begin reading his most famous book, *Charlotte's Web*, to your class.)

12TH GEORGE EASTMAN, inventor of the camera and founder of the Eastman Kodak Company, was born on this day in 1854. (Ask your students to each bring in a photo of themselves to display on a class bulletin board.)

13TH The first trans-Atlantic telephone conversation via TELSTAR was completed on this day in 1962. (Students might be interested in knowing how satellite communications work in both television and telephone.)

14TH Today is BASTILLE DAY! This celebration honors the victory of the people during the French Revolution in 1789. (Ask students to find the city of Paris on the class map.)

15TH REMBRANDT VAN RIJN, famous old master Dutch artist, was born on this day in 1606. (Bring some prints of Rembrandt's beautiful paintings into your classroom.)

16TH APOLLO 11 was launched on this day in 1969, with astronauts Collins, Armstrong and Aldrin. (Ask your students to locate Cape Canaveral, FL, on your classroom map.)

17TH APOLLO 18 and the U.S.S.R. craft SOYUZ 19 linked up in space in a dramatic gesture of goodwill in 1975. (Ask your students what other ways nations could promote peace and goodwill.)

18TH JOHN GLENN JR., American astronaut and politician, was born on this day in 1921. (Ask students to find out the particulars of his historic flight.)

19TH The first WOMEN'S RIGHTS CONVENTION was held on this day in Seneca Falls, New York in 1848. (Ask students to list some rights that women now have that they did not have then.)

20TH The first LANDING ON THE MOON by American astronauts Neil Armstrong and Buzz Aldrin was accomplished on this day in 1969. (Ask your students to find out what Armstrong said when he first set foot on the moon's surface.)

21ST British explorer MUNGO PARK began his voyage down the Niger River in Africa on this day in 1796. (Ask your students to trace his route on the class map.)

22ND EMMA LAZARUS, American poet who wrote the poem engraved on the Statue of Liberty, was born on this day in 1849. (Read her famous poem to your students.)

23RD The ICE CREAM CONE was introduced at the World's Fair in St. Louis by Italo Marchioni in 1903. (Treat your students to an ice cream treat on this summer day.)

24TH Today is MORMON PIONEER DAY, celebrating the founding of their settlement in Salt Lake City, Utah, in 1847. (Have students locate the Great Salt Lake on the classroom map.)

25TH Franklin D. Roosevelt was the first U. S. president to visit the islands of HAWAII in 1934. (Discuss the customs and dress of the people in Hawaii and hold a class luau.)

26TH NEW YORK STATE was the eleventh state to ratify the constitution and become a state, on this day in 1788. (Ask your students to name the other twelve states that made up the original thirteen.)

27TH U.S. figure skater PEGGY FLEMING was born on this day in 1948. (Ask your students to find out which year she won her Olympic gold medal.)

28TH British children's author BEATRIX POTTER was born on this day in 1866. (Read one of her charming stories to your class during quiet time.)

29TH CHARLES, PRINCE OF WALES and LADY DIANA SPENCER were married in St. Paul's Cathedral in London on this day in 1981. (See if your students know the identities of these two people and ask them to locate London on the classroom map.)

30TH HENRY FORD, American automobile manufacturer, was born on this day in 1863. (Ask your students to design a futuristic car.)

31ST THOMAS EDISON received a U.S. patent for his phonograph on this day in 1877. (Ask students about later advances in this invention and how technology may change it in the future.)

DON'T FORGET:

JULY IS NATIONAL ICE CREAM MONTH!

AUGUST

1ST FRANCIS SCOTT KEY, American author of the "Star Spangled Banner," was born on this day in 1779. (Start your class with the singing of the national anthem.)

2ND The first LINCOLN PENNY was introduced on this day in 1909. (Start a class collection of pennies and have students take turns rolling them into 50¢ rolls. When enough are collected, hold a class field trip.)

3RD CHRISTOPHER COLUMBUS set sail from Spain on his first voyage to the New World on this day in 1492. (Ask your students to trace his route on the the classroom map.)

4TH The DECLARATION OF THE RIGHTS OF MAN was adopted in France on this day in 1789. (Ask your students what rights should be included in such a document.)

5TH NEIL ALDEN ARMSTRONG, the first man to set foot on the moon, was born on this day in 1930. (Ask your students if they would ever like to travel to the moon or Mars.)

6TH The first atomic bomb was dropped by the United States on HIROSHIMA, Japan on this day in 1945. (Ask your students to discuss their feelings about nuclear weapons and how we might eliminate them from the world.)

7TH The nuclear-powered submarine NAUTILUS completed a historic voyage on this day in 1958. (Ask your students what was so unusual about this fantastic voyage.)

8TH Today is INTERNATIONAL CHARACTER DAY! (Hold a class discussion about what constitutes good character and morals.)

9TH The AUSTRALIAN GOLD RUSH began when a large gold nugget was discovered in New South Wales on this day in 1851. (Ask your students to find out more about both the California and Australian Gold Rush.)

10TH President Harry S. Truman signed the National Security Act, creating the DEPARTMENT OF DEFENSE on this day in 1949. (Ask your students to find out more about the duties of the Defense Department.)

11TH Today marks the "NIGHT OF THE SHOOTING STARS!" (Encourage your students to observe the night sky and count the number of falling stars (meteors) they see.)

12TH KATHERINE LEE BATES, author of the poem "America the Beautiful," was born on this day in 1859. (Ask your students to write their own poem about America.)

13TH Construction of the BERLIN WALL began on this day in 1961. (Explain to your students how this wall divided Germany and the city of Berlin. Ask them to find out when and why the wall was torn down!)

14TH Today is VICTORY DAY! This day celebrates the ending of World War II with the surrender of the Japanese in 1945. (Ask your students what other days might be considered "Victory Day!")

15TH The PANAMA CANAL was opened on this day in 1914. (Locate the canal on the class map and discuss how it has benefitted world trade and travel.)

16TH GAS STREET LIGHTS were introduced for the first time in London on this day in 1807. (Hold a class discussion about what life must have been like in the early 1800s.)

17TH American frontiersman DAVY CROCKETT was born on this day in 1786. (Arrange for a showing of one of Disney's "Davy Crockett" films in celebration.)

18TH VIRGINIA DARE, the first English child born in colonial America, was born on this day in 1587. (Ask students to find out more about the first group of colonists that came to America.)

19TH Today is NATIONAL AVIATION DAY and birthdate of ORVILLE WRIGHT, in 1871. (You might want to invite a pilot to your class to talk about his/her love of flying.)

20TH REINHOLD MESSNER, of Italy, was the first successful solo climber of MT. EVEREST, in 1980. (Ask your students to find out the altitude of the world's highest mountain.)

21ST HAWAII became the 50th U.S. state on this day in 1959. (Serve your class a treat of fresh pineapple in celebration.)

22ND The INTERNATIONAL RED CROSS was established in Geneva, Switzerland on this day in 1864. (Students might like to contribute, as a class, to this worthwhile organization.)

23RD American dancer and choreographer GENE KELLY was born on this day in 1912. (Encourage your budding dancers to demonstrate their talents to the class.)

24TH On this day in 79 A.D., MT. VESUVIUS erupted in southern Italy. (Older students might like to mark existing volcanos on the classroom map.)

25TH LEONARD BERNSTEIN, American composer and conductor, was born on this day in 1918. (Students might like to listen to his music from "West Side Story" and relate it to teenagers today.)

26TH The 19th AMENDMENT to the U.S. Constitution was ratified on this day in 1920. (Have your students find out what this amendment gave us.)

27TH Humanitarian MOTHER TERESA was born on this day in 1910. She won a Nobel Peace Prize, in 1979, for her work with the poor in India. (Ask your students to locate India on the classroom map.)

28TH Today marks the anniversary of the MARCH ON WASHINGTON in 1963. (Find a copy of Martin Luther King's speech "I Have a Dream" and read it to the class.)

29TH U.S. Senator STROM THURMOND set a filibuster record of speaking for 24 hours, 27 minutes on this day in 1957. (Ask your students to find out what he talked about.)

30TH The Space Shuttle DISCOVERY made its maiden flight on this day in 1984. (Ask students to find out about the Space Shuttle and how this type of space flight is different from the Apollo flights.

31ST MARIA MONTESSOR, the developer of the Montessori method of education, was born on this day in 1870. (Celebrate by simply having a great back to school!)

July

Sunday	Monday	Tuesday	Wednesday	Thursday	Friday	Saturday

August

Sunday	Monday	Tuesday	Wednesday	Thursday	Friday	Saturday

Mini Calendar Symbols

TF0700 July & August Idea Book

Summer Activities!

TF0700 July & August Idea Book

Summer Activities!

I'M GOING ON A PICNIC...

Have your students go on an imaginary picnic with this memorization game.

Have students sit in a circle on the floor. One student starts by saying, "I'm going on a picnic, and I'm taking apple pie and baked beans!" The third student then says, "I'm going on a picnic, and I'm taking apple pie, baked beans, and cupcakes!" The game continues around the circle with each student using the order of the alphabet for their answer and at the same time remembering what the other students have added. Any student that misses loses his or her place in the circle and sits out the rest of the game.

SUN PRINTS

Everyone has noticed how construction paper fades when left on a bulletin board a little too long. Use this effect of the sun in your next art lesson.

Give each student a dark sheet of construction paper. (Purple, blue or brown work best.) Ask the children to cut shapes from paper or arrange other flat objects on the paper with small pieces of tape or *Post-It* glue sticks. Tape the sheets, face out, to a sunny window. In a day or two, take the collages down and have students carefully remove the items. The construction paper under the shapes will remain dark while the rest of the paper will be faded.

A FIELD OF SUNFLOWERS

Give each student a small, yellow paper plate. Cut numerous flower petals from yellow and or gold construction paper and have the students glue the petals to the outer edge of the paper plate. When dry, give each child a handful of sunflower seeds and instruct them to glue the seeds to the center of the flower. Attach a long green paper stem and leaves to each child's sunflower and post them on the class board for a fantastic summer display.

QUICKIE SUMMER ACTIVITIES

Insect Spy - Find an insect in your backyard such as a honeybee, ant or a spider. Observe it closely. Does the bee collect nectar? Are the ants taking food back to the colony? Is the spider spinning a web or waiting for its next meal? Write about what you see.

Picnic Lunch - Pack a picnic lunch and invite a friend over to have lunch under a tree in a park or your own backyard.

Sky Observer - Ask your parents to take you someplace where the night sky can be observed. A country road or hilltop that has no artificial light offers the best views. Look for and identify the various planets, constellations and occasional shooting star!

Road Trip - If your family is planning a trip, locate the intended route on a highway map. Note the various towns and points of interest you will pass or have the opportunity to visit. Calculate the time it will take to make the trip. (If you can't take an actual trip, plan an imaginary one!)

Summer Jobs for Kids!

Kids love to earn their own money! Children learn the values of being resourceful and responsible. They also learn the benefits of saving money and planning ahead for spending it.

Discuss with your students ways they can earn their own money during the summer. You might encourage them to think of ways they can help or be of assistance to family members and/or neighbors. Here are a few ideas to get them started:

- Wash cars
- Mow lawns
- Walk or feed dogs
- Run errands
- Water plants
- Pull weeds
- Sweep porches
- Plant flowers
- Tutor a younger child in reading or math
- Collect and cash in recycled items

Have children select a "job" they would like to pursue. Instruct them to list the necessary plans and materials they would need to begin doing the "job." They should also calculate prices they will charge and the estimated time it will take to accomplish.

My Summer Job! _____
                                    Name

Type of job: _____

Needed Materials: _____

_____

_____

_____

Needed Tools: _____

_____

_____

_____

Amount I will charge: _____

_____

Time it will take: _____

Describe in detail your summer job. _____

_____

_____

_____

Stay Cool! Visit the Library!

Dreams come true when you READ!

DISCOVER LIBERTY IN THE LIBRARY!

_____
Student's Name

Did a great job today!

Date _____ Teacher _____

_____
Student's Name

was SUPER today!

Way to Go!

Teacher _____ Date _____

_____
Student's Name

Did a "Yummy" Job!

Teacher _____ Date _____

was a real winner today!

Teacher _____ Date _____

Pencil Toppers

Reproduce these "Pencil Toppers" onto index or construction paper. Color and cut out. Use an art knife to cut through the Xs.

Slide a pencil through both Xs, as shown.

Use as classroom, holiday or birthday treats.

TF0700 July & August Idea Book

My Summer Book!

Name _____

TF0700 July & August Idea Book

Sunglasses!

Children will love making and wearing these fun sunglasses!

Cut the patterns from heavy paper. Carefully cut out the lenses. Cut circles of colored cellophane and paste them to the backs of the glasses. Attach the bows to the frame by fitting them into the designated slots.

Decorate the sunglass frames with feathers, glitter or sequins.

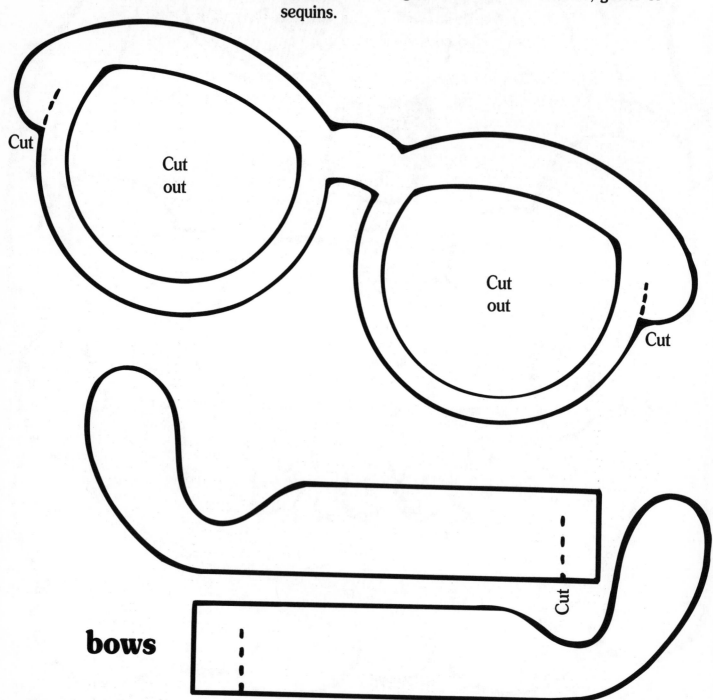

Giant Summer Glasses!

Have each student cut this giant glasses pattern from folded construction paper.

Instruct the students to write about a summer adventure in one lens and draw a picture of the activity in the other.

Display the glasses on the class board to motivate the children into pursuing a summer hobby or taking swimming or music lessons.

Title the display, "Looking Forward to a Great Summer!"

FOLD

My Summer Journal!

Date: _____

What happened: _____

_____

_____

My feelings!: _____

_____

_____

Date: _____

What happened: _____

_____

_____

My feelings!: _____

_____

_____

Date: _____

What happened: _____

_____

_____

My feelings!: _____

_____

_____

Attach the patterns to a
small paper lunch bag.

Sunshine Puppet!

You Are My Sunshine!

Award students yellow paper sun rays that they can paste to their own "You Are My Sunshine!" sun pattern.

Students collect all eight rays and then display the suns on the class board!

Date

Teacher

You Are My Sunshine!

Name

38

Watermelon, Pizza & Ice Cream!

TF0700 July & August Idea Book

Watermelon, Pizza and Ice Cream Activities!

If you ask children to list their favorite foods more than likely they will mention watermelon, pizza or ice cream! Here are a few motivational activities that use these fun foods to help reinforce language arts, mathematics and other areas of your own curriculum.

ICE CREAM VOCABULARY

Ask your students to brainstorm all of the words they would use to describe their favorite flavor and texture of ice cream. Children can write poems or short stories using the descriptive words.

As a creative twist, ask students to write a descriptive account of someone eating an ice cream cone. Tell them that they cannot use the following words: ice cream, cone, lick, cold and delicious.

FAVORITE FLAVORS

The International Ice Cream Association list the most popular flavors in this order: vanilla, chocolate, butter pecan, strawberry, Neapolitan, chocolate chip and French vanilla. List these flavors on the class board and ask your students to vote for their favorite flavor. Does your class rank the flavors in the same order?

Children may wish to write to the International Ice Cream Association for more information. Their address is

888 Sixteenth Street N.W.,
Washington, D.C. 20006.

WATERMELON IDEAS

Try one of these refreshing ideas next time your students need a break from routine classwork.

• Ask students to discover how watermelons are grown and where they originated. Some students may like to find out how large they can grow.

• Pass out pieces of watermelon for the students to enjoy. Ask them to save the seeds. Dry them overnight and plant them the next day. In a couple of weeks you should find small watermelon plants coming up.

• Cut several slices of watermelon from red and green construction paper. Write a number or simple math problem on each slice. Save real watermelon seeds from a class picnic and have students glue the appropriate number of seeds to the watermelon slices.

• Make watermelon ice. Cut chunks of watermelon, minus the rind and seeds, and use a blender to puree. Pour into individual cups and chill in the freezer until icy. Eat on a hot summer day.

• Write the word W-A-T-E-R-M-E-L-O-N vertically on the class board. Ask children to use each individual letter to start a sentence on why they like summer or picnics.

Watermelon, Pizza and Ice Cream Activities!

PIZZA PUZZLES

Use the pizza slice pattern in this chapter to create a clever matching activity or fascinating learning puzzle.

Eight pizza slices, arranged in a circle, make a complete pizza pie. Copy and cut the pizza slices from brown or red construction paper. On the slices write vocabulary words, contractions, synonyms, math problems, ordinal numbers, etc. Keep the pizza slices in a clean pizza box. Students can take the boxes to their desks and independently arrange the pizza slices in the correct order or groups.

You can easily teach fractions of halves, quarters and eighths by using the same pizza slices.

WATERMELON POEMS

Cut a large, red and green slice of watermelon from construction paper for each child in class. You may want to make them on a fold, creating watermelon booklets. Children can write "mouth-watering" poems or summarize short stories on the melons. Display them on the class board as a refreshing summer display.

ICE CREAM FACTS

Ask students to research the many ways ice cream has made history! Suggest they find out the following:

- Who was the first to invent ice cream?
- How did the early settlers make ice cream?
- Who was the first to serve ice cream in the White House?
- Who was the first to manufacture ice cream?
- How was the first ice cream soda invented?
* How did the ice cream "sundae" get its name?
- When and where was the first ice cream cone invented?
  - How much ice cream is produced in the United States each year?

MELON MANIA

Bring a variety of different melons into the classroom for your students to sample. Make sure you include watermelon, cantaloupe, honeydew and casaba melon.

Ask your students to describe the tastes and textures of each one.

You may also want to have your students sample pickled watermelon rind and ask them to explain its characteristics.

CREATIVE PIZZA WRITINGS

Ask your students to brainstorm as many pizza toppings as possible. Write their responses on the board and ask them to use the toppings in a creative poem or short story.

Watermelon, Pizza and Ice Cream Activities!

TOASTER OVEN PIZZAS

Let students have the fun of making their own mini pizzas using a toaster oven and these simple ingredients.

Instruct students to wash their hands and then give each student one canned refrigerator biscuit. Tell them to flatten out the biscuit like a small pancake and place it onto a square piece of tin foil. Each student can then spread a spoonful of ready-made pizza sauce on their pizza followed by grated cheese and assorted toppings. Bake each pizza six to eight minutes at 400 degrees.

WATERMELON FRACTIONS

Create a visual watermelon display to help explain fractions to your students.

Cut several large green circles from construction paper and the same number of red circles, only slightly smaller. Glue the red circles to the centers of the green circles to create melon rounds.

Cut the melon rounds into the desired fractions, such as; halves, quarters, thirds, etc. Children can help make the pieces look more like watermelon slices by gluing on real watermelon seeds or drawing them on with a black felt marker.

As a special treat, let your students cut their own real watermelon rounds into specified fractions. Eating the melons can be the prize for a job well done.

YUMMY FIELD TRIPS

Take your students on a fun field trip to the local ice cream shop or pizza parlor. Contact the parents and shop owners several weeks in advance. They will probably insist that the visit take place before the shop opens in the morning hours. Encourage the owner's participation in the learning process of the visit. They may suggest that groups of students make their own pizza or sundaes. Suggest that the shop owners give the children coupons that can be taken home to parents to promote their particular business.

HOMEMADE ICE CREAM

Ice cream will taste that much sweeter when your students have helped make it using a hand-crank ice cream freezer. Here is a simple recipe:

> 1 can condensed (sweetened) milk
> 1 qt. whole milk
> 12 oz. frozen whipped topping
> 4 cups mashed bananas, strawberries or peaches

Pack the freezer with crushed ice and freezer salt. Have students take turns turning until the mixture thickens. Serve in small paper cups with plastic spoons. Enjoy!

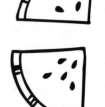

Ways to Use Ice Cream Cones in the Classroom!

• **CLASS MONITORS** Write jobs on paper cones and students' names on paper ice cream scoops. Pin the cones to the class board with the title, "We've Got the Scoop on Classroom Jobs!" Students can help move the individual student ice cream scoops from cone to cone.

• **BOOK REPORTS** Give each student one paper cone and three paper ice cream scoops when they finish reading their next library book. Have them write the title of the book and the author's name on the first scoop, a list of characters on the second scoop and a summary of the story on the third scoop. Students can write their own names on the cones and pin the completed "book report-ice cream cones" on the class board.

• **READING GROUPS** Label paper cones with your specific reading group names on the class board. Write the name of every student on paper ice cream scoops. Stack the scoops on the appropriate cone to show which student is in which reading group.

• **CLASS RULES** Display a large paper cone on the class board labeled with your name and room number. Write specific rules you wish your students to follow on paper ice cream scoops. Stack the scoops on the cone for a fun reminder of your expectations.

• **STUDENT AWARDS** Give each student his or her own paper cone and tell them to pin it to the class board. Students earn ice cream scoops cut from colored paper as they accomplish goals or improve behavior. Children will love seeing who can stack the most ice cream scoops.

• **MULTIPLICATION RECOGNITION** Give each student a paper ice cream cone that is displayed on the class board. As each student demonstrates his or her knowledge of a multiplication table, offer a paper ice cream scoop labeled with the number of the table demonstrated. Kids will grow in pride and motivation as the ice cream cones grow in height.

Matching Ice Cream Cones

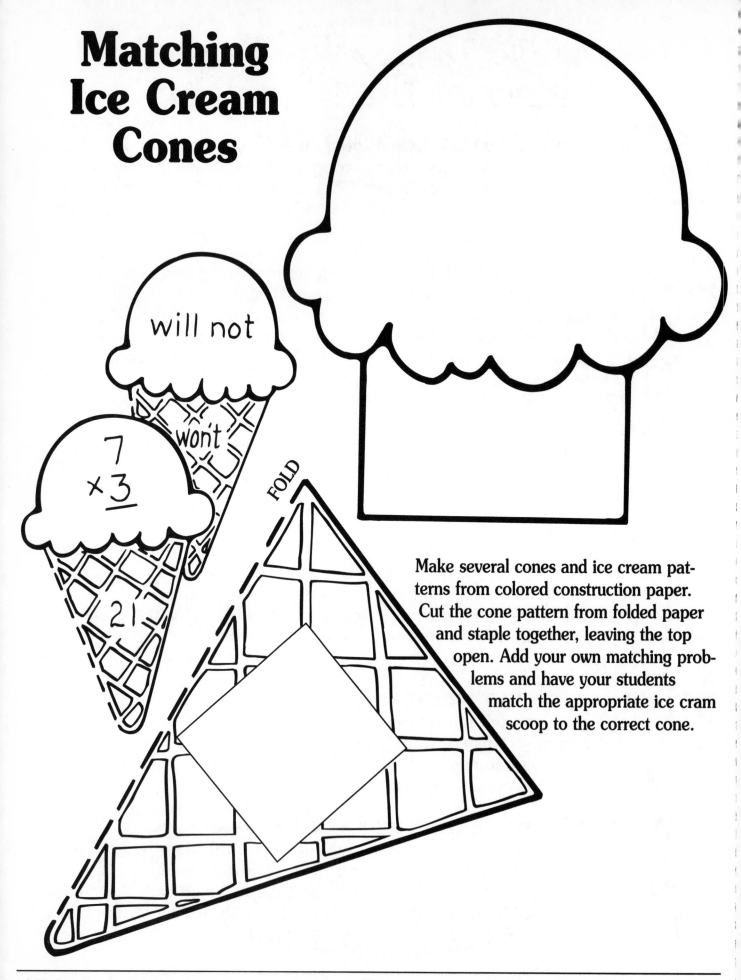

will not

won't

7
×3
___

21

FOLD

Make several cones and ice cream patterns from colored construction paper. Cut the cone pattern from folded paper and staple together, leaving the top open. Add your own matching problems and have your students match the appropriate ice cram scoop to the correct cone.

TF0700 July & August Idea Book

Ice Cream Cone Puppet

Cut out and paste these patterns to a small lunch bag to make a cute puppet.

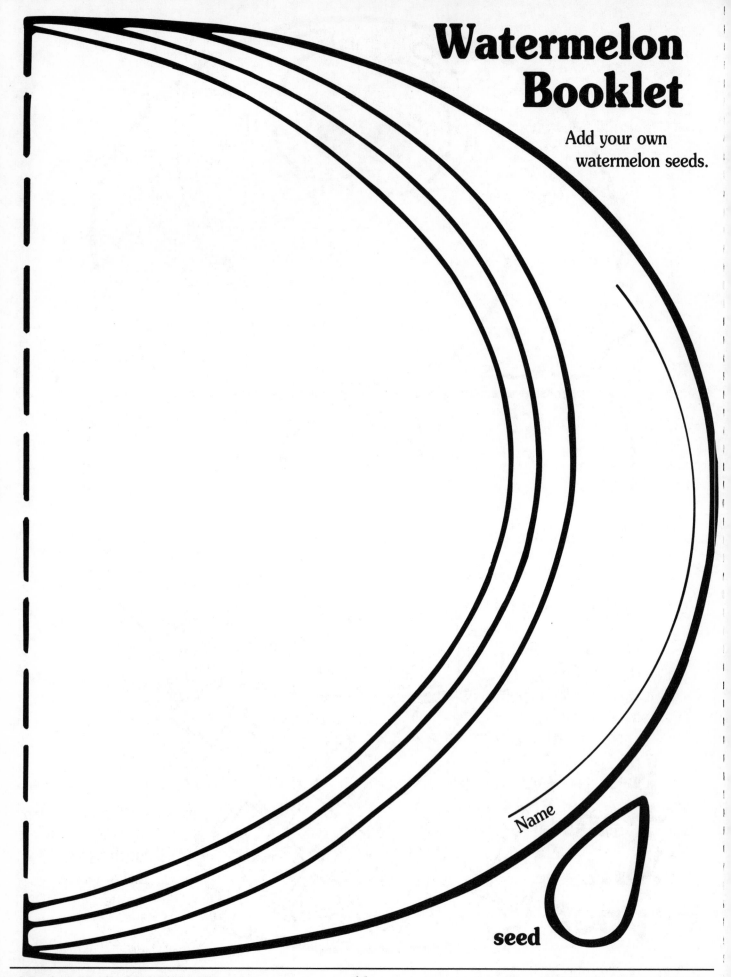

Watermelon Booklet

Add your own
watermelon seeds.

Name

seed

Watermelon Slices

Use this watermelon slice pattern in a variety of activities.

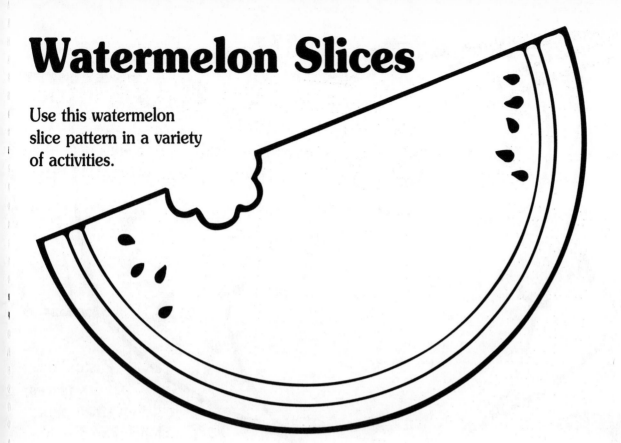

• Make watermelon name tags for the year-end class picnic.

• Make a variety of matching games. Questions on one half, answers on the other.

• Cut the top off of a small milk carton and glue a watermelon half to each side. Fill the box with crayons, paper clips, loose change or a collection of shells or marbles.

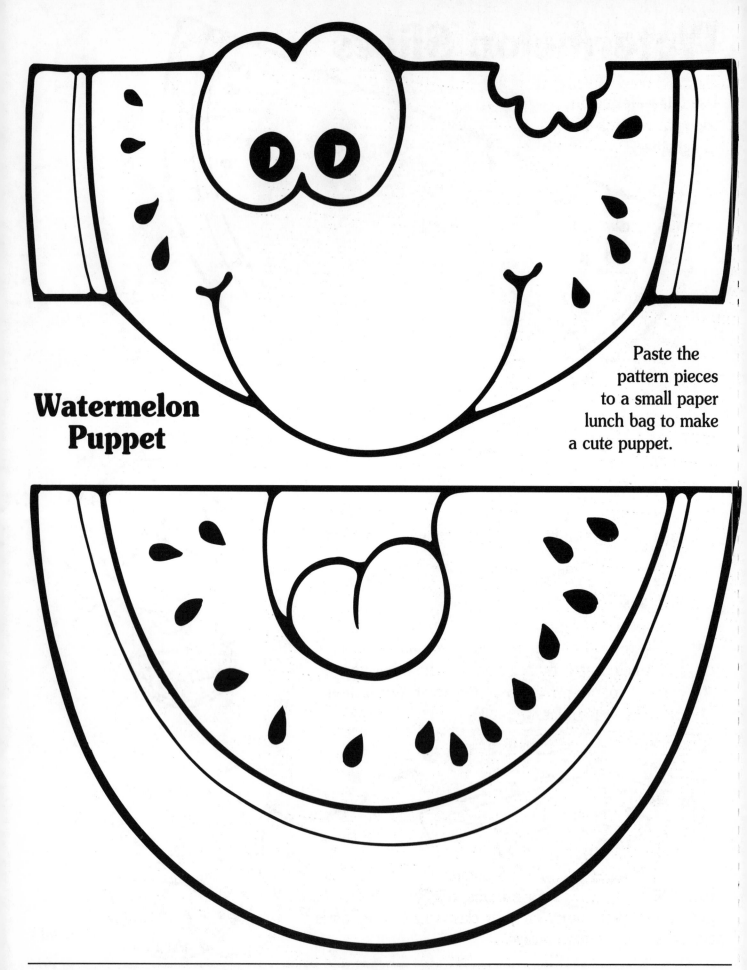

Watermelon Puppet

Paste the pattern pieces to a small paper lunch bag to make a cute puppet.

Pizza Awards!

The next time you wish to award your students with an extra special treat, give them a piece of pizza!

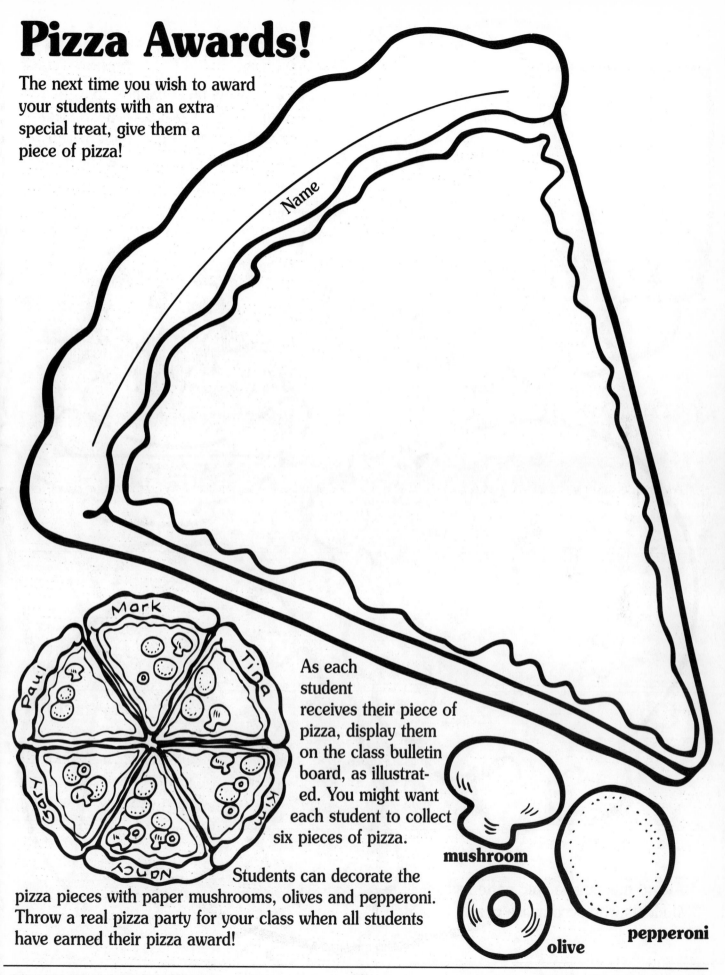

Name

As each student receives their piece of pizza, display them on the class bulletin board, as illustrated. You might want each student to collect six pieces of pizza.

Students can decorate the pizza pieces with paper mushrooms, olives and pepperoni. Throw a real pizza party for your class when all students have earned their pizza award!

mushroom

olive

pepperoni

Banana Splits!

Have students build banana splits as they accomplish goals or improve behavior. Give each student a dish pattern and instruct them to paste it to a sheet of construction paper.

Alisha

Award the banana split patterns to students who accomplish goals.

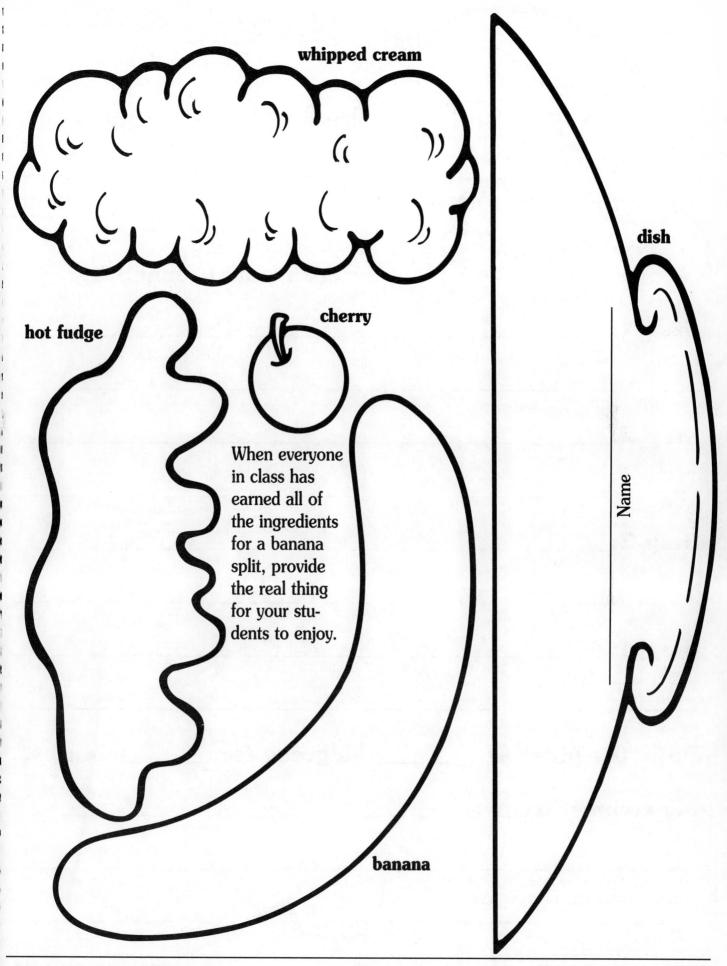

whipped cream

dish

hot fudge

cherry

Name

When everyone in class has earned all of the ingredients for a banana split, provide the real thing for your students to enjoy.

banana

My Pizza Recipe!

_____
Student's Name

My favorite type of pizza is:

_____

_____

Here's how to make it!

Step 1:_____

_____

Step 2:_____

_____

Step 3:_____

_____

Step 4:_____

_____

Bake the pizza at _____ **degrees for** _____ **minutes.**

My comments:_____

_____

_____

Pizza Chef!

Have students write creative pizza recipes or imaginary menus. Mount each paper on construction paper and display this "Pizza Chef" around the page!

Name

Ice
Cream
Booklet

4th of July!

TF0700 July & August Idea Book

Independence Day!

The most important patriotic holiday to all United States citizens is Independence Day, or the Fourth of July. Independence Day celebrates the historical signing of the Declaration of Independence by the Continental Congress on July 4, 1776. With this act, the thirteen colonies formed a new nation, the United States of America.

Celebrations continued for several days. The people of Philadelphia, Pennsylvania cheered as citizens spread the news that the Declaration of Independence had been signed. The Liberty Bell was rung at Independence Hall and a statue of King George III was taken down and destroyed. That night people lit bonfires and danced in the streets in celebration.

Today, the Fourth of July is celebrated with family picnics, parades, fireworks and political speeches. It is a happy, joyous time but also one in which we should all remember the sacrifices our forefathers made in order to give us this great nation.

DECLARATION OF INDEPENDENCE

The Declaration of Independence is a document that declares the rights of a new nation. It explains the feelings of the colonists and lists the wrongs they suffered under British rule. It also states that the people of the United States will fight their own wars, make their own peace and carry on their own trade. With the signing of this document, the United States became an independent, free nation.

The first person to sign the Declaration was John Hancock, president of the continental Congress. Thomas Jefferson, with the help of Benjamin Franklin and John Adams, wrote the document. Fifty-six men signed the declaration. In signing, each man pledged to his new country "our lives, our fortunes, and our sacred honor."

You might like to read a few sentences of the Declaration of Independence to your students.

"We hold these truths to be self-evident, that all men are created equal, that they are endowed by their Creator with certain unalienable Rights, that among these are Life, Liberty and the pursuit of Happiness. That to secure these rights, Governments are instituted among Men, deriving their just powers from the consent of the governed."

Patriotic Fun!

ACTIVITY 1   FIND THESE PATRIOTIC WORDS:

INDEPENDENCE	RIGHTS
DECLARATION	EQUALITY
LIBERTY	HONOR
JUSTICE	FREEDOM
PATRIOTISM	AMERICA
STARS	GLORY
STRIPES	FLAG
UNCLE SAM	

```
X C F T R E V F R E E D O M D F T Y
D F L D T Y G H J U S E T E O U L K
F Y A R G T Y J U S T I C E D E W R
W O G F G T Y H J U I K L O P H J S
P A T R I O T I S M S W Q E R T Y T
S D F R T G G D E D S E W D S W T A
F B V C X L T Y U I L I B E R T Y R
D C V F G O G T H D E S E S A E T S
F B V C X R F A M E R I C A D R E T
C V B F G Y D R E F G T H Y U J K R
U N C L E S A M D R F G T Y H J U I
H S D R R E G V B N M J H K I U J P
O G D E C L A R A T I O N D F R T E
N F V G B H N J M K L O I K J M N S
O V B G F B A Z J H R I G H T S G L
R C V B H G N M J K L O I K M J N H
Q R I N D E P E N D E N C E P L M T
Z E Q U A L I T Y M X P O L T R F E
```

WRITE A PARAGRAPH ABOUT FREEDOM USING AT LEAST FIVE WORDS IN THE PUZZLE ABOVE.

ACTIVITY 2
WHO'S HIDING IN THESE NUMBERS?

___ ___ ___ ___ ___ ___ ___ ___ ___

___ ___ ___ ___ ___ ___ ___.

       TF0700 July & August Idea Book

Paste these eagle patterns onto a small paper lunch bag to make a 4th of July puppet.

My Liberty Book!

FOLD

Name _____

59

What Liberty Means to Me!

4th of July Visor

Copy this "4th of July" visor onto sturdy index or construction paper. Children can do the coloring.

Punch holes at both ends and attach string elastic or mailing string. (With elastic, the students can easily remove the visors without retying.)

Uncle Sam

Use these "Uncle Sam" patterns to display patriotic papers.

Happy Birthday U.S.A.

TF0700 July & August Idea Book

4th of July Finger Puppets!

Freedom Name Plate!

Happy 4th of July!

_____
Name

Freedom Mobile

Cut these patterns from heavy paper and hang with string or fishing line.

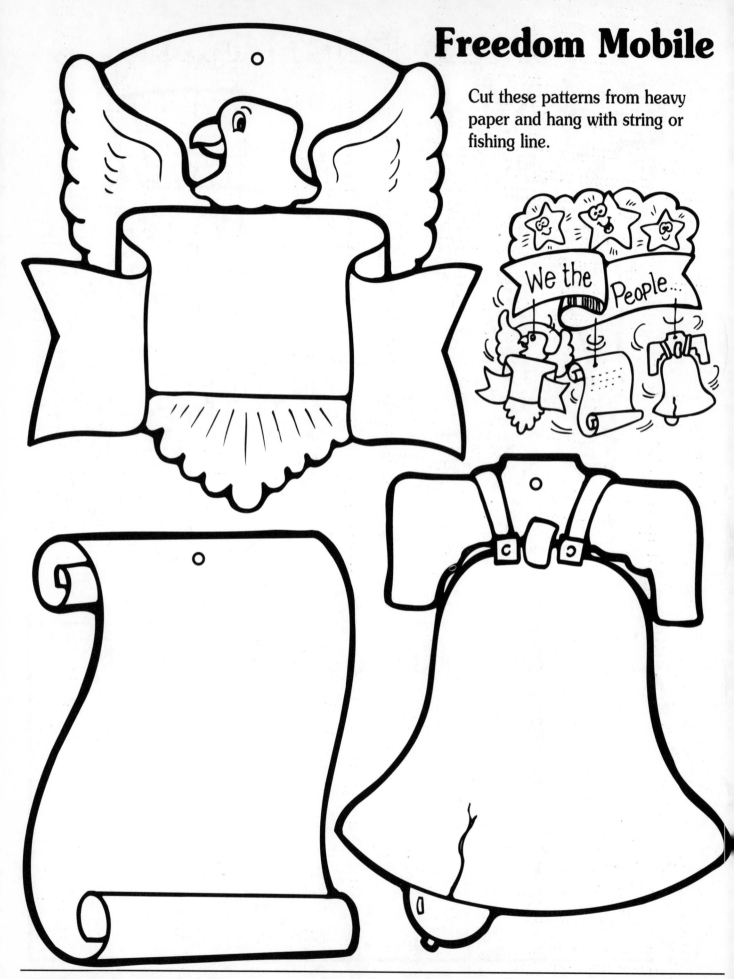

My Freedom Fighter Report!

Student's Name _____

Freedom Fighter's Name: _____

_____

Birthdate: _____

Birthplace: _____

Here is how this person helped promote freedom:

_____

_____

_____

_____

People who benefited from this person's actions: _____

_____

_____

This person's most important contribution: _____

_____

_____

_____

My thoughts: _____

_____

_____

_____

_____

The Wild West!

Wild West Activities!

Bring the fun and excitement of the "Wild West" with these creative activities!

COWBOY STORIES

Ask your students to write a creative story about the old West. You may want to list the following words on the class chalkboard and ask them to pick several of the words to use in their story.

bandit	bedroll
boots	bunkhouse
camp fire	canyon
cattle	cattle drive
chaps	chuck wagon
corral	cowboy
cowpoke	coyotes
deputy	desert
dude	herd
holdup	horses
Indians	lasso
longhorns	outlaw
posse	ranch
range	rodeo
rope	round-up
rustler	saddle
saloon	sheriff
six-shooter	stampede
stagecoach	trail
wagon train	wolves
wrangler	vittles

RODEO TIME

Dedicate one of those hum-drum days of summer to "Class Rodeo Day!"

Tell your students a few days in advance that they may dress like cowboys or cowgirls on this special day. Arrange some of these fun activities:

"Sharp Shooter Spelling Bee"
"Jump Roping Contest"
"Bronco Relay Race"
"Lariat Ring Toss"

Award star-shaped "Sheriff Badges" to all the participants!

THE LIFE OF A COWBOY

Ask your students to research what a day in the life of a cowboy would have been like.

Start out by sending them to the library to research the early years of the cattle business. They may write about the "cattle drives," "round-ups," and "harvest." On the classroom map have them show the four main cattle trails: the Sadalia Trail, Chisholm Trail, Goodnight-Loving Trail and the Western Trail.

Some students may want to record what a cowboy wore and ate on the trail. Other students may want to explain the procedures for branding calves. You may want to assign one student to report on the effect of the sheep industry on the cattle business.

As the project comes to a close, hold a real cowboy barbecue in the classroom. A serving of chili and beans and a small slice of cornbread will inspire in any student a feeling of the Old West!

WANTED POSTERS

Give each student their own wanted poster to complete. Ask them to draw a picture of themselves in the space provided or paste in a school photo. Display the posters on the class bulletin board as a way for students to learn more about their fellow classmates.

Wild West Activities!

FAMOUS CHARACTERS

The Old West offered a variety of notorious characters who played a big role in the romance of the age. Your students might find it fun to discover the truth about these legendary "real" people. Here are a few names they might like to research:

The Outlaws
> Billy the Kid
> Calamity Jane
> Butch Cassidy
> Kid Curry
> Bob, Emmett and Grafton
Dalton
> Pearl Hart
> Tom Horn
> Frank and Jesse James
> Belle Starr

The Law
> Ira Aten
> Wyatt Earp
> Wild Bill Hickok
> Bat Masterson
> Zeke Miller
> John Slaughter
> Tom Smith
> Heck Thomas

The Showmen/women
> William F. Cody
> Annie Oakley
> Nat Love

HORSE VOCABULARY

List several of these words or phrases on the class board and ask students to use them in a "horsy" writing assignment.

Riding Tall In the Saddle
Hold Your Horses
From the Horse's Mouth
Horse Of a Different Color
Horse Around
Horse and Buggy

Horseback	Horsepower
Horsefly	Horseshoes
Horsehair	Horsewhip
Horselaugh	Horse Sense

FAMOUS HORSES

Students might like reading about horses in the school library. Several books will give them information about famous horses as well as general knowledge about riding and care. Some horses are famous because they belonged to U.S. Presidents, others won national races and still others belonged to television characters. Ask your students to research a famous horse and give an oral report to their classmates. Here are a few suggestions:

Trigger	Buttermilk
Seabiscuit	Black Beauty
Fury Mister Ed	
Silver	Flicka
Man 'O War	Secretariat

A VISIT BY A HORSE

In most areas, it is possible to arrange for someone in the community to bring a horse to your school for a visit. Even in large cities, you may be able to arrange for a policeman on horseback or carriage driver to visit your classroom.

Ask your students to prepare a variety of questions before the visit. Here are a few suggestions:

Height and weight of the horse?
Name and age?
How it is groomed?
Where does it sleep at night?
Is ite a work horse?
Does it wear horseshoes?
What equipment is needed to ride?
What training is needed to ride?
What does it eat?

Even if a real horse is unavailable, you might ask someone who owns a horse to bring pictures and a saddle to show the children.

Walk, Cantor, Trot and Gallop!

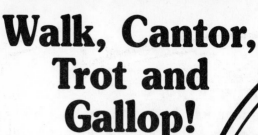

The four gaits of a horse are walk, cantor, trot and gallop. Use these terms in your next activity to motivate your students in accomplishing assigned goals.

Copy these four different horseshoe awards each labeled with the four gaits. When a student completes the first part of a goal, he or she is given a "walking" award.

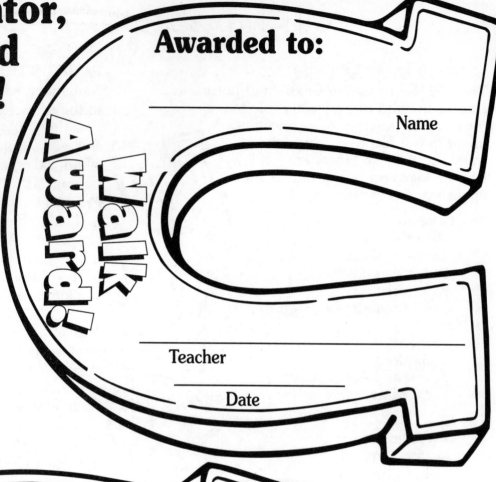

Awarded to:

_____
Name

Walk Award!

_____
Teacher

_____
Date

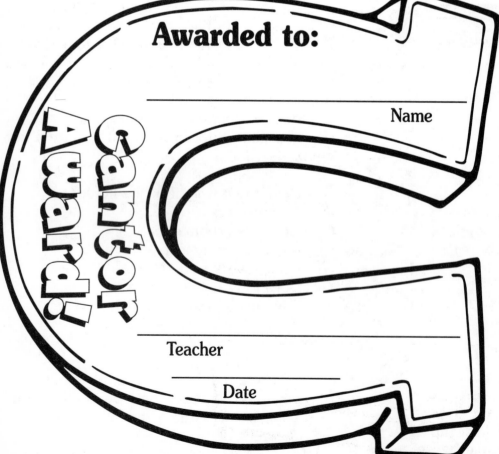

Awarded to:

_____
Name

Cantor Award!

_____
Teacher

_____
Date

After completion of the second stage, the student wins a "Cantor," and so on. Upon completing the goal, the student is declared to be at full speed and is given the "gallop" award.

Students that collect all four horseshoes can display them on the class board under the tile "These Students Have Horse Sense!"

When all of the students have accomplished their goals, hold a class party. Since horses love oats, oatmeal and brown sugar would make a perfect treat!

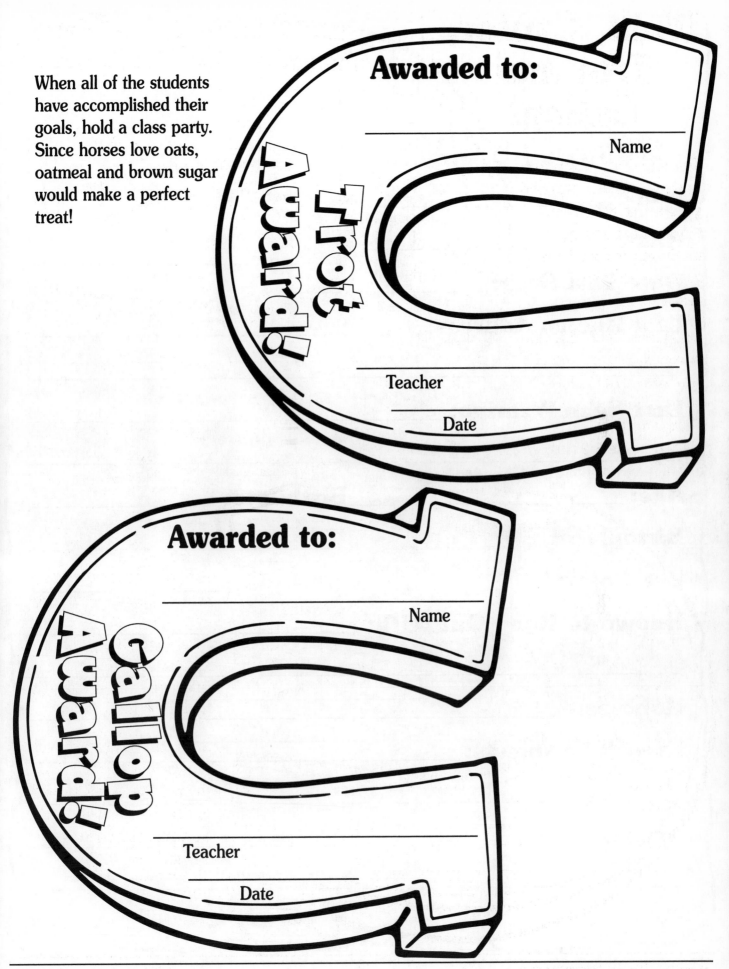

Awarded to:

_____
Name

Trot Award!

Teacher

Date

Awarded to:

_____
Name

Gallop Award!

Teacher

Date

WANTED

$1,000,000 REWARD!

Name: _____

Alias: _____

Picture

Date Last Seen: _____

Last Known Address: _____

_____

Last Seen Wearing: _____

_____

Age: _____ Birthdate: _____

Birthplace: _____

Eye Color: _____ Hair Color: _____

Known to Hang Out With: _____

_____

Hobbies: _____

Favorite Subjects: _____

_____

Accused of: _____

_____

Horse Character

Enlarge this humorous horse and display it around the edge of your next bulletin board. Entitle the board, "*These Students Don't Horse Around!*"

TF0700 July & August Idea Book

Cowboy-Cowgirl Hat Pattern

Cut this pattern from colored paper and attach it to a paper head band.

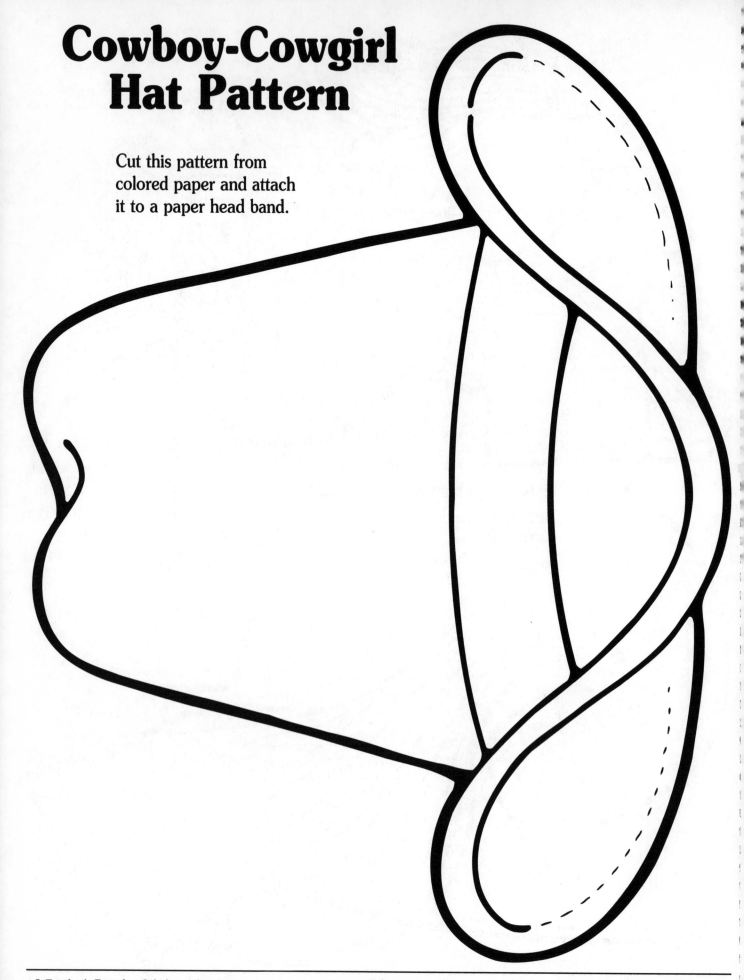

TF0700 July & August Idea Book

Sheriff Badge and Spurs

Have your students bring hats, kerchiefs, boots, etc. to school for a special "Cowboy Dress-Up Day!" They can enhance their costumes with these simple patterns.

SHERIFF

_____
Name

The badge can be cut from yellow paper and pinned to a shirt or vest. Cut two spur patterns from folded construction paper. Staple one together at the spur and carefully slip it over the top of your boot or shoe.

FOLD

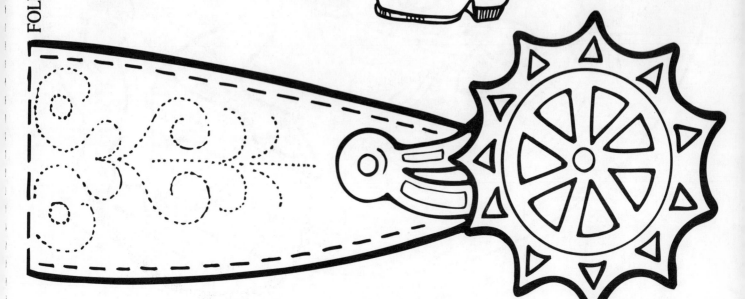

Cowboy Wheel

Copy this cowboy Wheel" onto heavy
index paper. Color, cut out and
assemble with brass fasteners. Add
your own problems and answers. Move
the horse's tail to reveal the answer.

Cut Out

Cut Out

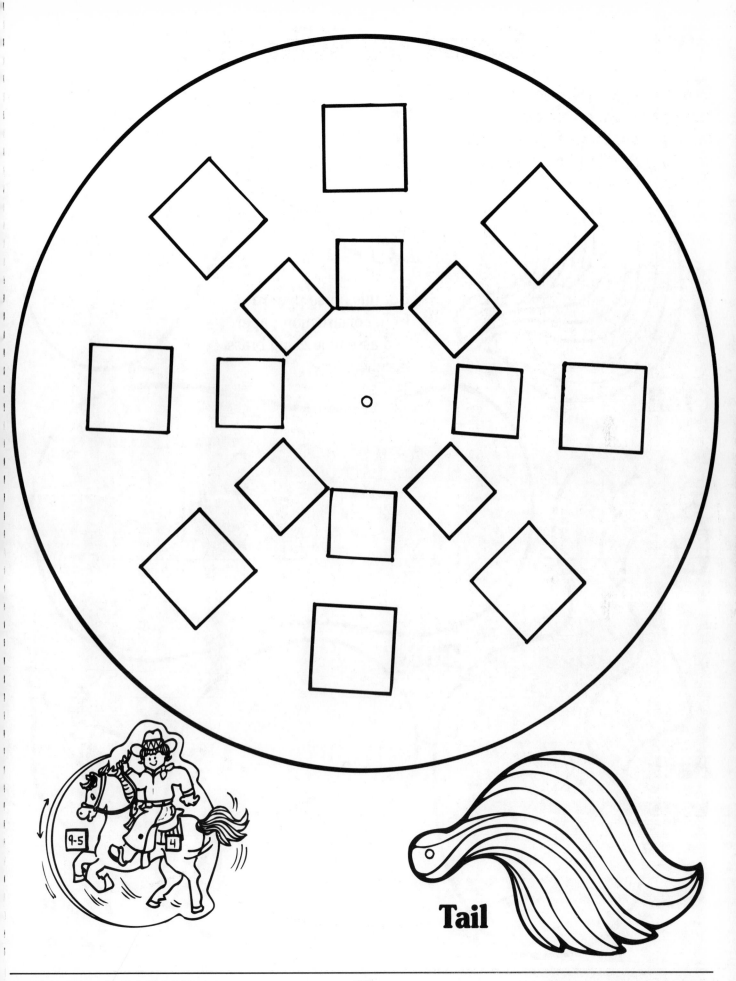

Tail

Movable Horse

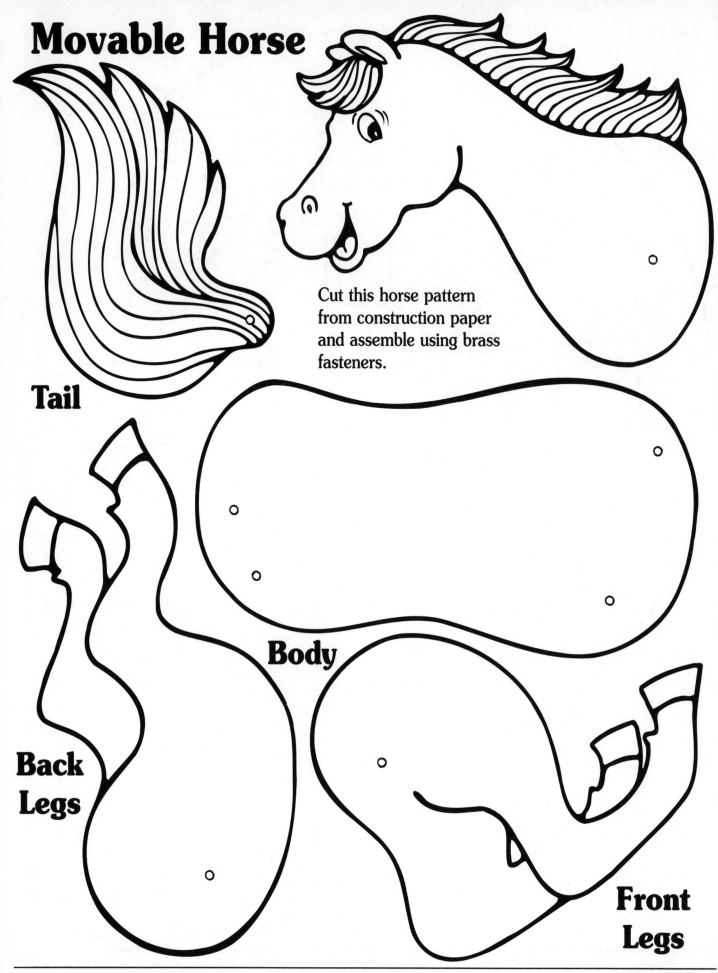

Cut this horse pattern from construction paper and assemble using brass fasteners.

Tail

Body

Back Legs

Front Legs

TF0700 July & August Idea Book

The Wild West!

Name _____

Reading Round-Up!

Book Title: _____

_____

Author: _____

Main Characters: _____

_____

_____

The Main Story: _____

_____

_____

_____

_____

_____

_____

_____

I liked the book... ☐ **yes**   ☐ **no**

Why? _____

_____

_____

_____

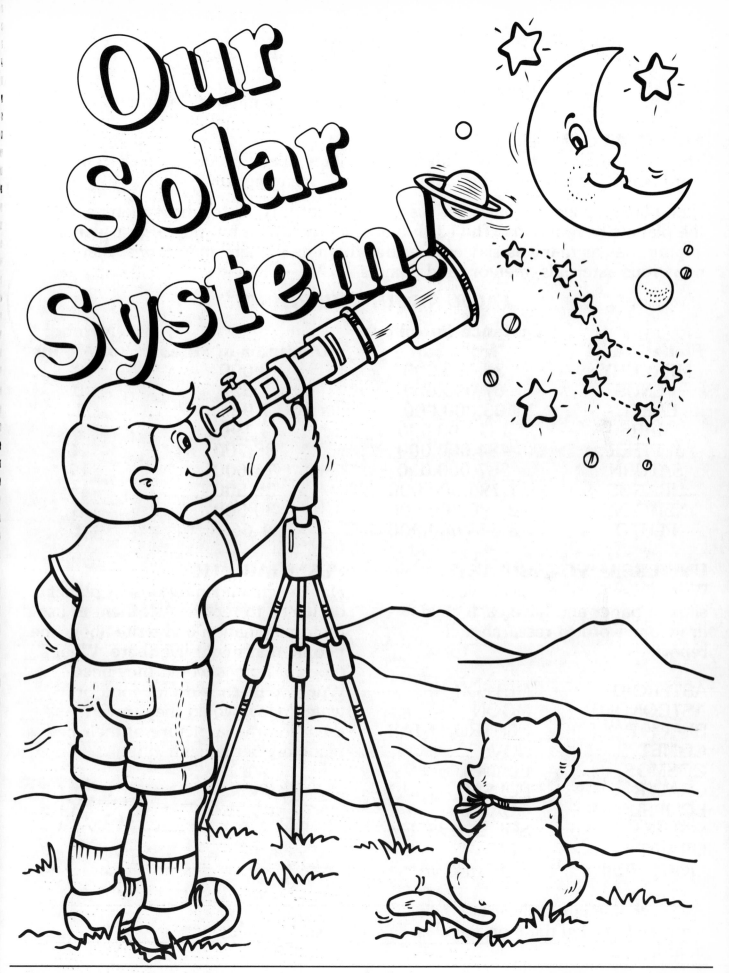

Our Solar System!

Exploring Our Solar System!

Try some of these activities to reinforce a space unit in your classroom.

SOLAR INFORMATION

The sun and all the planets, with their satellites, make up our solar system. The word "solar" comes from the Latin word "sol," meaning sun.

Nine planets make up our solar system. The earth is one of these planets. Six of the planets have moons. The earth has only one moon but the largest planet, Jupiter, has as many as sixteen. Besides the nine planets and moons, there are numerous asteroids, meteors and comets.

FACTS ABOUT THE PLANETS

Planet Name	Distance (in miles) from Sun	Diameter in Miles	Number of Moons
MERCURY	36,300,000	3,009	0
VENUS	67,000,000	7,522	0
EARTH	93,000,000	7,926	1
MARS	141,400,000	4,196	2
JUPITER	484,000,000	88,700	16
SATURN	887,000,000	74,600	17
URANUS	1,784,000,000	32,500	15
NEPTUNE	2,796,000,000	30,500	8
PLUTO	3,668,000,000	1,660	1

UNIVERSAL VOCABULARY

Write these "astronomical" words on slips of paper and have each child draw one word to research and report.

ASTEROID	METEOR
ASTRONOMY	MOON
BLACK HOLE	NEUTRON STAR
COMET	NOVA
COSMOS	PLANET
CRATER	PULSAR
ECLIPSE	QUASAR
GALAXY	SOLAR SYSTEM
GRAVITY	STAR
LIGHT YEARS	SUPERNOVA

Ask each student to illustrate their word and display them on the class board.

PLANETARY TRIP

Have each student choose a planet on which to report. Ask them to use their imagination and write about the people that might live there. What types of homes would they need? What would they do for food or water? How would they travel? Ask them to draw a picture of their new planetary settlement.

Exploring Our Solar System!

MEMORIZING PLANETS

Teach your students an easy way to memorize the planets of our solar system with this simple trick. Ask them to memorize this sentence.

"MY VERY ENERGETIC MOTHER JUST SWALLOWED an UGLY, NASTY PICKLE!"

Show them how each word gives a clue to the order of the planets.

MERCURY, VENUS, EARTH, MARS, JUPITER, SATURN, URANUS, NEPTUNE, PLUTO

This type of memory technique is called a "mnemonic sentence." Ask students to write other "mnemonic" sentences to help them memorize all kinds of things.

SPACE INFORMATION

NASA provides materials and resources for teachers about astronomy. They also publish a teacher's newsletter specifically for classroom use. Write to:

NASA
Educational Publications Services
XEP
Washington, DC 20546

The National Air and Space Museum also provides information. Write to:

National Air & Space Museum's
Educational Resource Center
Office of Education, P-700
Washington, DC 20560

SOLAR SYSTEM DISPLAY

Accurately display the planets along a classroom wall or corridor by using these ideas and dimensions.

Using these measurements, the sun would have to be more than 15 feet in diameter. With this in mind, simply note the location of the sun and begin with the first planet, Mercury!

MERCURY - Place Mercury (1 3/4 inches in diameter) 2 inches from the sun.

VENUS - Place Venus (3 1/4 inches in diameter) 3/4 inches from the sun.

EARTH - Place Earth (2 inches in diameter) 4 1/2 inches from the sun.

MOON - Place the Moon (1/2 inches in diameter) as close to Earth as possible.

MARS - Place Mars (1 inch in diameter) 7 inches from the sun.

JUPITER - Place Jupiter (20 inches in diameter) 25 inches from the sun.

SATURN - Place Saturn (18 inches in diameter) 44 inches from the sun.

URANUS - Place Uranus (8 inches in diameter) 89 inches from the sun.

NEPTUNE - Place Neptune (7 inches in diameter) 140 inches from the sun.

PLUTO- Place Pluto (5/8 inches in diameter) 183 inches from the sun.

Ask students to cut the planets from colored paper and draw in the particular characteristics of each one. Have them add moons, asteroids, rings, etc. Have them also research and label the accurate sizes and distances of each planet.

Exploring Our Solar System!

ASTRONOMICAL QUESTIONS

Here are a few nighttime questions you may want your students to research:

What's the difference between a planet and a star?

Can you name all the planets in our solar system in order?

What is a "blue moon"?

What is the Milky Way?

How large is the moon and how far is it from the earth?

Is there a "man in the moon"?

What is a shooting star?

Students may also like to research one of the seven original American astronauts or one of the many constellations.

SOLAR HEAT

Help your students experience the sun's heat with this fun activity.

Give each student two 12 inch sheets of aluminum foil. Have them place the two pieces of foil together and carefully cut out two mitten shapes. (The mittens should be much larger than their own hands.) Instruct them to tape the front and back of each mitten together.

Students wear the mittens outside on a sunny day. Ask them to hold the mittens so that the sun's rays reflect on their faces. Very soon, they will feel the heat of the sun. Discuss with them other ways people can capture the sun's energy.

ROCKET TO THE SUN

Demonstrate to your students the great distances of space and at the same time give them some practice at figuring miles per hour and distances traveled.

During the first week of school, tie a 30' length of yarn or heavy string across the top of your classroom. Hang a paper earth at one end of the string and a paper sun at the other end. Attach a paper rocket to the string at planet Earth. Each day (or week), move the rocket the distance traveled using the formula below. (Attach the rocket with a clothespin so it can be easily moved.)

Tell your class that the average speed of the rocket will be about 17,500 miles per hour. At that speed, the rocket can travel 420,000 miles per day, or about 1 1/2 inches.

The sun is approximately 93,000,000 miles from the earth. At this rate, the rocket will not reach the sun for 240 days. Remind the students that a real rocket would also take as long.

Older students can figure how many miles the rocket will travel in a week, month, etc.

Exploring Our Solar System!

PHASES OF THE MOON

Is there daytime and nighttime on the moon? Of course there is! And seeing them from here on earth gives us a variety of views as the moon rotates around the earth. What we see is called the phases of the moon.

Ask your students to consult almanacs, newspapers or a calendar to begin their study. Every night, have them view the moon and determine its phase. Ask them to also note the time the moon rises and from which direction.

Children should draw a picture of the moon each night. Most nights, they will be able to see a slight change. Continue with the study for 29 nights so they can witness the entire cycle of the moon.

Ask them to learn these phases of the moon and label their pictures accordingly:

NEW MOON - The moon is invisible
WAXING CRESCENT - first thin sliver
FIRST QUARTER - half moon
WAXING GIBBOUS - 3/4 moon
FULL MOON
WANING GIBBOUS -3/4 moon
LAST QUARTER - half moon
WANING CRESCENT - last thin sliver
NEW MOON (invisible moon again!)

THE BIG DIPPER

Make a miniature planetarium to help youngsters find the big dipper in the night sky.

Cover one end of an empty toilet tissue tube with black paper and tape in place. Gently poke holes in the black paper to resemble the big dipper. Have the children hold up the tube to the light and look through the end. Light will shine through the holes and show the famous constellation.

FOLLOW THE SUN

Let your students measure the movements of the earth in relation to the sun with this easy activity.

On a sunny day, turn the lights down in the classroom. Instruct your students to notice a deep shadow on the classroom floor. Ask one student to make the shadow line with a piece of making tape. The time should be written on the tape. After ten minutes, ask another student to make another shadow line. Repeat the experiment several items throughout the day. Ask students to measure the distance between the pieces of tape.

Hold a class discussion on what these measurements mean.

STAR GAZERS

Cut several stars from yellow construction paper. Write a vocabulary word on each star. Attach a string to each star and hang them all from the ceiling. Children can choose several words to use in their next creative writing assignment.

You may also choose to write words that can be rhymed on each star. Children gaze at the stars and write as many rhyming words as possible. The student with the most rhyming words could win a small prize.

Star Puzzle

Make several copies of this star pattern on index or construction paper. Write your own math problems on each star point, as shown. Write the answers on the center of the star. Cut off all five points of the star and place the star pieces in an envelope. Have the individual students take the envelope to his or her desk and assemble the star, answering the problems correctly. This is a great way to practice multiplication facts.

Create a starry bulletin board by asking the children to pin the completed star puzzles to the classroom board. Add a rocket ship or astronaut character to the board.

Space Fun!

ACTIVITY 3   UNSCRAMBLE THESE PLANET NAMES.

htaer _ _ _ _ _

toupl _ _ _ _ _

neutpne _ _ _ _ _ _ _

suevn _ _ _ _ _

urcyerm _ _ _ _ _ _ _

nusaru _ _ _ _ _ _

rnutsa _ _ _ _ _ _

piertuj _ _ _ _ _ _ _

rasm _ _ _ _

ACTIVITY 4   PLACE THE PLANET NAMES IN ORDER.

1. _____   4. _____   7. _____

2. _____   5. _____   8. _____

3. _____   6. _____   9. _____

ACTIVITY 5   FIND THESE SPACE WORDS.

ASTRONOMY
ORBIT
TELESCOPE
PLANETS
COMET
ASTEROID
STAR
METEOR
MOON
SATELLITE
ASTRONAUT
SHUTTLE

```
S W E R D S H U T T L E D R E W Q G H Y T
D O D C V F G T R E W S C B G Y T U I P O
S R H Y A S T R O N A U T D E R C Y T H U
C B Y H U J I Y N M H Y T R F R O D R E T
D I S A T E L L I T E D R E R F M G T Y U
S T E L E S C O P E F R V S G T E U I P L
A S D F C V B G T R E D A T D E T F E W S
M E T E O R D R E F R G E A F E W Z X V B
O D E R F H T R W F G B H R R D W C V G H
O D R E A S T E R O I D F V B G H Y T N M
N F R E S D G B F T R E W Q A D F R T G H
K L P L A N E T S T G H Y U N M J K I U H
D C V G F T Y H J A S T R O N O M Y V C X
```

Solar System Mobile

You can make a variety of mobiles with these planet patterns. Each child might wish to make their own, or you could simply arrange the planets on the class bulletin board.

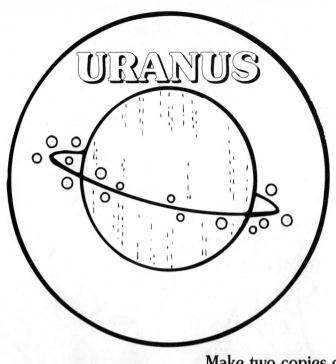

URANUS

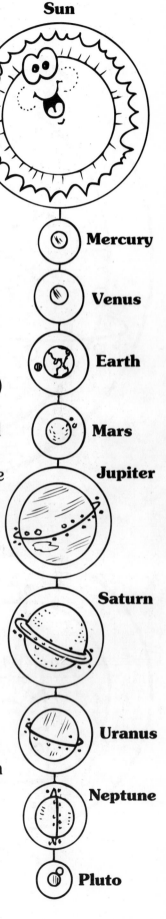

Sun

Mercury

Venus

Earth

Mars

Jupiter

Saturn

Uranus

Neptune

Pluto

MERCURY

VENUS

Make two copies of each planet and sun pattern and color with crayons. Cut out each pattern piece. Glue each planet (back to back) down a long piece of string or yarn. Position the planets, in the order of their orbit, around the sun. Hang the mobile from the class ceiling, or have each child make their own mobile and hang it in their room at home.

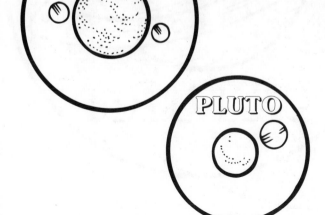

MARS

PLUTO

This planet mobile can also be arranged horizontally. Attach the planets along a piece of yarn, as described above. The display will reach from one side of your class-room to the other if you space the planets apart according to scale.

TF0700 July & August Idea Book

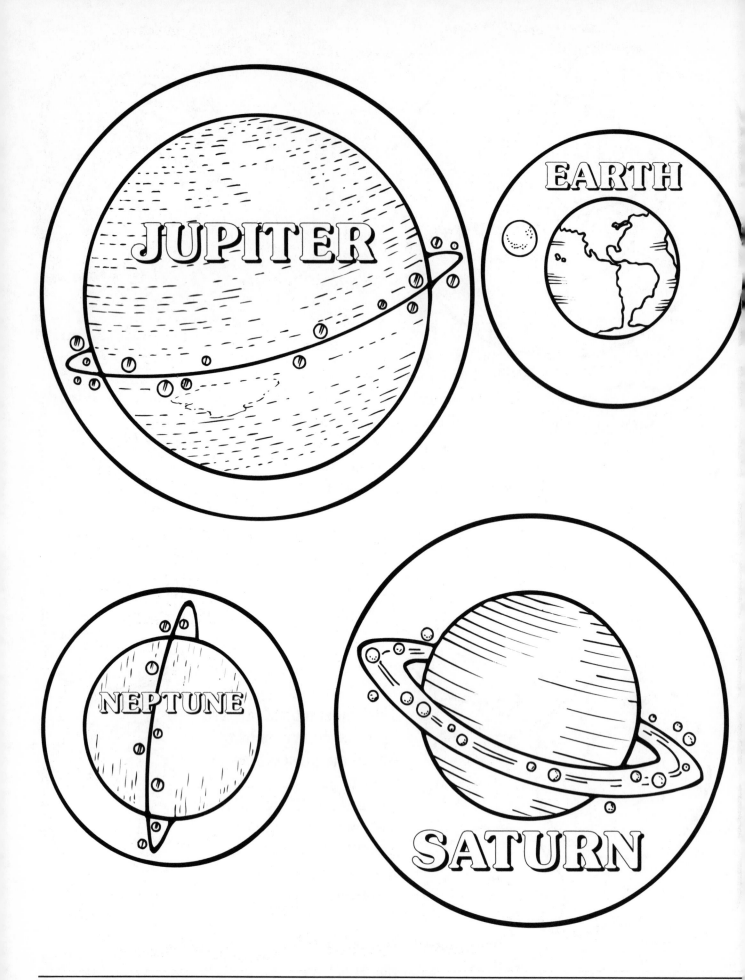

Name

Martian Mania!

Celebrate the planet Mars by declaring the day "Martian Mania Day!"

Ask your students to come dressed in their silliest clothes. They might wear mismatched patterns or sweaters turned inside out.

Have children make these simple Martian antennae. Glue a paper star or planet on the end of each pipe cleaner. Glitter can be added to the stars for a dazzling effect. Clip the antennae to their head by clipping them in place with hair clips.

Serve Moon Cookies (sugar cookies) and Martian punch, as a treat in the afternoon.

Solar System Bingo!

This bingo game offers an exciting way for your students to learn about our solar system. Give each child a copy of the space bingo words listed below or write the words on the class chalkboard. Ask your students to write any 24 words on his or her bingo card. Use the same directions you might use for regular bingo.

SPACE BINGO WORDS

SUN	NEPTUNE	STAR	DISCOVERY	FLIGHT	CHALLENGER
MERCURY	PLUTO	PAD	ASTRONOMY	UNIVERSE	OXYGEN
VENUS	MOON	METEOR	ASTRONAUT	CREW	GALAXY
EARTH	ORBIT	SATELLITE	SHUTTLE	LUNAR	NOVA
MARS	TELESCOPE	SOLAR	GRAVITY	NASA	SPHERE
JUPITER	PLANETS	SYSTEM	ATMOSPHERE	APOLLO	AIR
SATURN	COMET	SPACE	COUNTDOWN	EXPLORER	OBSERVATORY
URANUS	ASTEROID	ROCKET	VOYAGE	LAUNCH	CONSTELLATION

SOLAR SYSTEM BINGO

FREE

Astronaut Wheel

Copy this "Astronaut Wheel" onto heavy index paper. Color, cut out and assemble with brass fasteners. Cut out the two boxes, as shown.

Add your own math problems and answers to the wheel on the next page. Move the flag to reveal the answers.

Cut Out

Cut Out

TF0700 July & August Idea Book

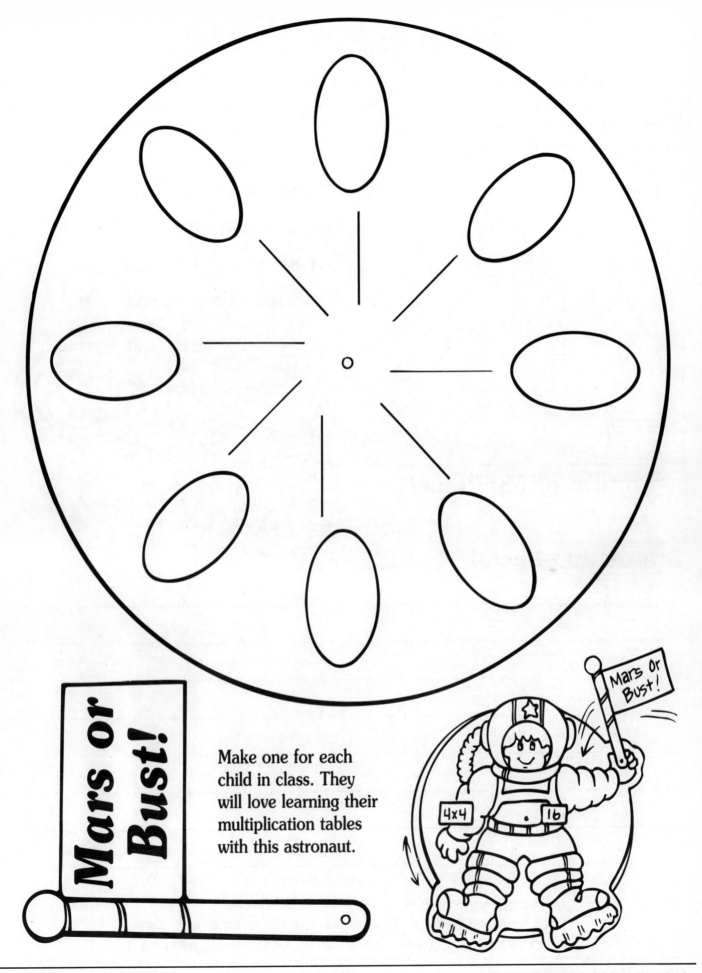

Make one for each child in class. They will love learning their multiplication tables with this astronaut.

Mars or Bust!

4x4 16

Mars or Bust!

TF0700 July & August Idea Book

My Planet Report!

Student's Name

Planet: _____

Distance from Sun: _____

Size/Diameter: _____

Number of Moons: _____

Surface Temperature: _____

Picture of My Planet!

Interesting Facts!

_____

_____

_____

_____

_____

_____

_____

_____

(On a separate piece of paper write a story of what it would be like to visit this planet.)

Out of This World World Award!

_____
Name

has accomplished

_____

_____

_____   _____
Date   Teacher

Space Name Tag

Reproduce this name tag pattern on colored paper. Award them to kids when they complete their study of the solar system.

Name

       TF0700 July & August Idea Book

Astronaut

Let's Eat Nutritiously!

Nutrition Activities!

MENU NUTRITION

Collect a variety of menus from coffee shops, restaurants and fast food places. Ask students to select a menu and choose a meal that would be nutritious and low in fat. Have them also select the most unhealthy item on the menu.

Students may like to write their own menus listing only healthy meals. Have them use the nutrition pyramid as a guide.

RECOGNIZING VEGETABLES

Let your students practice their memorization skills and vegetable knowledge with one of these familiar games.

- Place a variety of vegetables on a tray. Make sure you include some that are a bit unusual. Give the students several minutes to carefully study the vegetables. Remove the tray and ask the students to list as many of the vegetables they can remember. The student with the most correct vegetables wins.

- Cut pictures from seed catalogs or use the vegetable cards included in this unit. Pin one picture to the back of each student. Make sure the student does not see or its name. Each student may then ask other students to help identify the vegetable by asking them only yes or no questions. Award students with a fresh carrot when they guess their vegetables.

VEGETARIANS

Many people of the world eat little or no meat. Some people choose to be vegetarians for health reasons, some because they do not want animals killed and others because meat is so expensive. Whatever the reason for not eating meat, it is still important to eat enough protein for a healthy body. Most vegetarians get their protein from legumes such as peas and beans.

Ask your students to plan and illustrate a vegetarian meal. Instruct them to include the various food groups, substituting meat with protein substitutes.

UPSET THE VEGETABLE CART!

Encourage listening skills and at the same time promote your students' vegetable awareness with this fun game!

Assign each student the name of a vegetable, making sure you give two or more students the same vegetable name. Call out the name of a vegetable. Students having that vegetable name must hurry and switch seats. After a few rounds, declare "Upset the vegetable cart!" With this, all students must quickly change seats. After a while, remove one seat and choose a student to be the vegetable caller. When the cue "Upset the vegetable cart!" is given the caller hurries to get a seat. The student left without a seat becomes the next caller.

Vary the game by calling out vegetable types such as root vegetables, leafy vegetables, or vegetables we eat as flowers.

Nutrition Activities!

NUTRITION CONCENTRATION

Two students can play a "Concentration Game" by using the food cards and the Nutrition Pyramid contained in this chapter. Lay all of the cards face down on a table top. Each player takes turns revealing two cards at a time trying to match one section of the Nutrition Pyramid. If the cards match, the player keeps the cards and draws again. Cards that do not match are returned to their exact spot and the player forfeits his or her turn to the other player. The game continues until all cards are matched. The player with the most cards wins the game.

GO FISH NUTRITION PYRAMID!

Give each player a copy of a Nutrition Pyramid. Make four copies of each food card (found in this chapter) and have each player draw five cards. Place the remining cards in a stack in the middle of the table. An example of play might be when player #1 asks player #2 if he or she has an "ice cream card." If player #2 has the card, he or she must give it to the first player. When player #1 collects all four ice cream cards, the cards are placed in the correct area of that player's nutrition pyramid. If player #2 does not have the card, the first player must "Fish" a card from the center stack. The game continues until one player has at least one matched set of cards for each area of his or her pyramid. The first player to achieve this wins the game!

NUTRITIOUS RECIPES

NUTRITIOUS CANDY

1 cup peanut butter
1/2 cup honey
1/4 cup sunflower seeds
1/4 cup wheat germ
1/4 cup dried skim milk
2 tsp. vanilla
crushed corn flakes or shredded coconut

Mix the first six ingredients together and shape into small balls. Roll the balls in the coconut or corn flakes. Refrigerate before eating. Makes about 40 small balls.

FUZZY BANANAS

1 pint sour cream or yogurt
1 banana for every four children
1 package shredded coconut
1 box of toothpicks

Spear the banana chunks with a toothpick and dip into the sour cream or yogurt, coating it thoroughly. Roll in the coconut and eat right away.

CARROT SALAD

1 carrot
4 tsp. raisins
2 tbsp. mayonnaise
4 tsp. chopped nuts

Carefully grate the carrot into a small mixing bowl. Add the other ingredients and stir together. Refrigerate or eat immediately.

Nutrition Pyramid

QUANTITY AND QUALITY!
Eating a balanced diet in moderation is key to a healthy life.

STEP TO EXERCISE
Get 30 to 60 minutes of moderate to rigorous exercise every day!

WHOLE-GRAIN CEREAL

GRAINS

WHOLE-GRAIN CEREAL

4-6 oz. Daily

VEGETABLES

1½ – 2½ Cups Daily

TF0700 July & August Idea Book

F R U I T S

1 – 1¹⁄₂ Cups Daily

M I L K

2-3 Cups Daily

O I L S

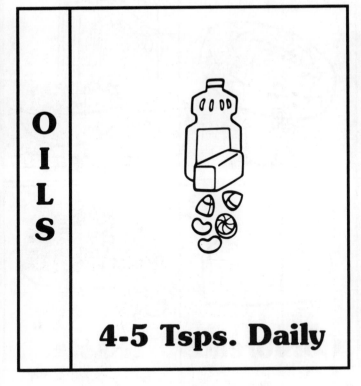

4-5 Tsps. Daily

M E A T & B E A N S

3-5 oz. Daily

Post the Nutrition Pyramid at home on the refrigerator door to remind yourself and family members of the importance of a balanced diet.

Cut these Nutrition Groups apart. Assemble them to form a Nutrition Pyramid on a large sheet of construction paper and paste in place. Color the illustrations any way you wish.

Turkey   **Eggs**   **Butter**   **Ice Cream**

Yogurt   **Candy**   **Candy**   **Bread**

Pretzel   **Muffin**   **Bagel**   **Cereal**

Rice   **Crackers**   **Cornbread**   **Pasta**

Food Cards

Try using these food cards one of these ways:

- Let students select a card and ask them to bring in that particular food for the other
    students to sample.
- Have students select a card to research. Instruct them to find out where and how the food is
    grown or how it is manufactured and/or processed.
- Tell students to categorize the cards into the groups shown on the Nutrition Pyramid.

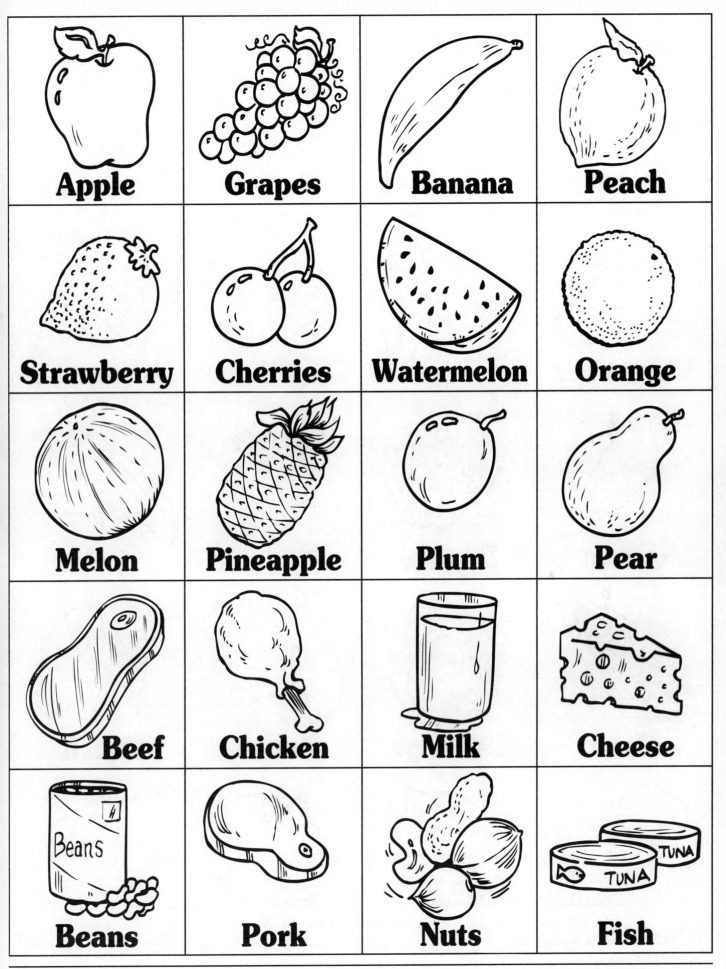

Apple	**Grapes**	**Banana**	**Peach**
Strawberry	**Cherries**	**Watermelon**	**Orange**
Melon	**Pineapple**	**Plum**	**Pear**
Beef	**Chicken**	**Milk**	**Cheese**
Beans	**Pork**	**Nuts**	**Fish**

 TF0700 July & August Idea Book

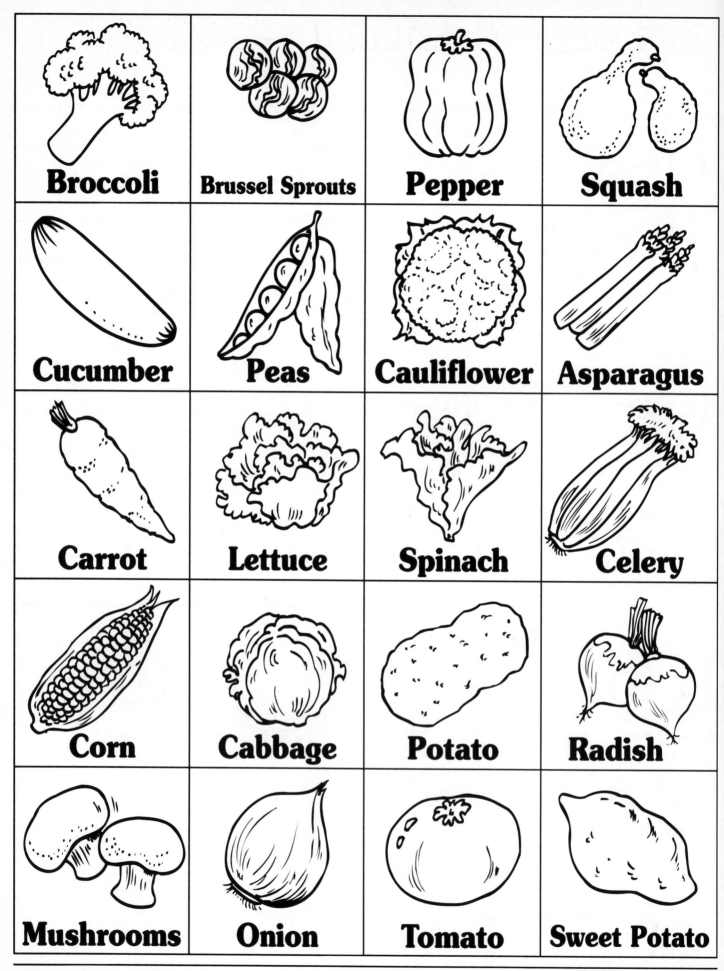

Broccoli **Brussel Sprouts** **Pepper** **Squash**

Cucumber **Peas** **Cauliflower** **Asparagus**

Carrot **Lettuce** **Spinach** **Celery**

Corn **Cabbage** **Potato** **Radish**

Mushrooms **Onion** **Tomato** **Sweet Potato**

TF0700 July & August Idea Book

Important Nutrients!

Vitamin A increases resistance to infection and improves eyesight.

_____

_____

_____

Vitamin B aids in good digestion and steady nerves.

_____

_____

_____

Vitamin C prevents scurvy and helps our muscles and gums.

_____

_____

Vitamin D helps keep our teeth and bones healthy and strong.

_____

_____

Carbohydrates give us strength and energy.

_____

_____

Fats, in correct amounts, enhance our skin and give us energy.

_____

_____

Proteins build and repair our bodies.

_____

Chef Costume

Make each of your classroom chefs their own chef's hat. Form a 10" high strip of white butcher paper into a cylinder for each student and tape it in place to fit.

Chef scarves can be cut from red paper or checkered gift wrap paper using the pattern below.

Cut cooking spoons from brown paper for each child in class!

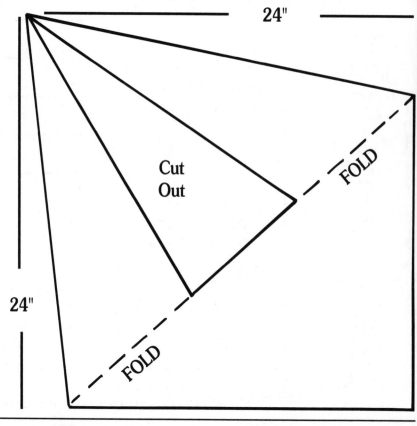

24"

24"

Cut Out

FOLD

FOLD

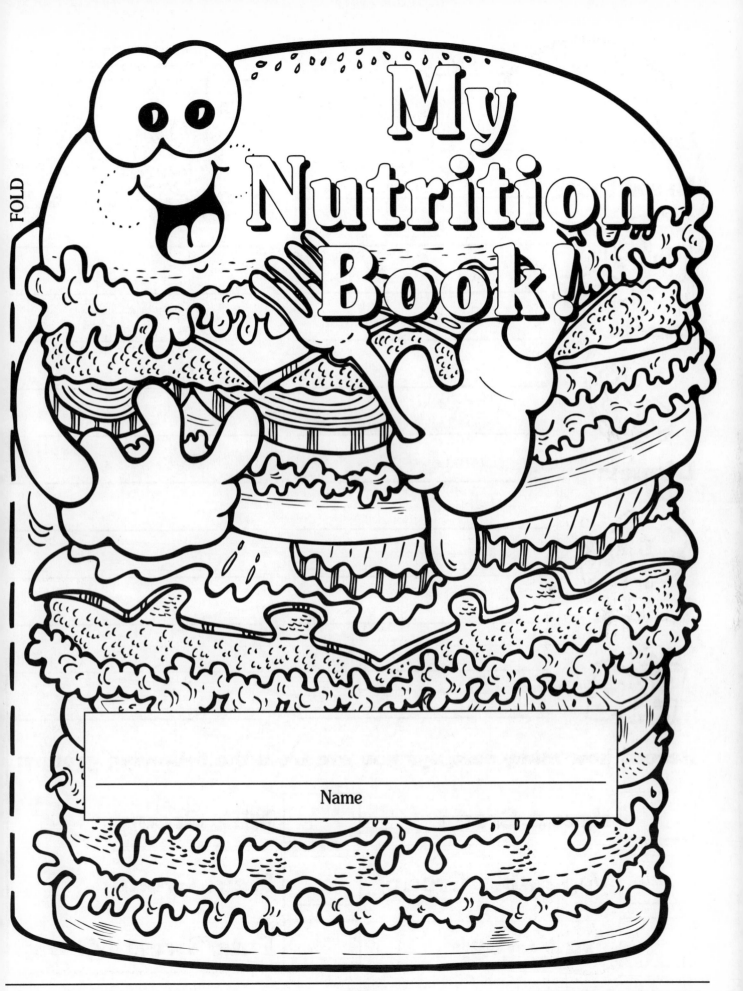

My Nutrition Book!

Name

FOLD

My Daily Diet!

Date: _____

Breakfast: _____

_____   _____

_____   _____

Lunch: _____

_____   _____

_____   _____

Dinner: _____

_____   _____

_____   _____

Snacks: _____

_____   _____

_____   _____

Record how many servings you ate from the following groups:

☐ **Bread Group**   ☐ **Milk Group**

☐ **Vegetable Group**   ☐ **Meat Group**

☐ **Fruit Group**   ☐ **Fats/Sweets Group**

A New Start!

A New Start for Back to School!

Begin the new school year in a way that will make learning fun for both you and your students!

CLASSROOM THEMES

Choose a theme for your classroom that you can use all year round! Use the chosen theme in depicting reading groups, class rules, class calendars, homework incentives, weekly and monthly awards, welcome bulletin board and much much more! Here are some suggested themes:

Airplanes
Alligators
Apples
Balloons
Bears and Bees
Beavers
Birds
Butterflies
Cookies
Cats
Clocks
Clowns/Circus
Crayons
Dinosaurs
Dogs

Dolphins
Dragons
Elephants
Farm Animals
Fish
Flowers
Footprints
Frogs
Hats
Horses
Ice Cream
Insects
Islands
Jungle
Kangaroos

Kites
Lady Bugs
Lions and Tigers
Mice
Monkeys
Octopus
Owls
Paint Brushes
Pencils
Penguins
Pigs
Pirates
Rabbits
Raccoons

Rainbows
Rockets
Seals
Shapes
Snakes
Spiders
Sun and Stars
Trains
Turtles
Umbrellas
Watermelons
Whales
Wishing Wells
Zoo Animals

(An index of themes found in the Teacher's Friend Monthly Idea Books can be found on page 143 of this book! Teacher's Friend also has Seasonal Clip Art Books that contain cute pictures of many of the themes listed.)

A New Start for Back to School!

OTHER WAYS TO USE YOUR THEME IN THE CLASSROOM:

- Create or buy a large door chart or poster welcoming your students to class.
- Send a thematic postcard home to each student a few days before school begins telling him or her your name, room number and how happy you will be to see them!
- Collect a variety of library books about your theme for a silent reading area.
- Find and prepare the materials to make a simple thematic craft with your students on the first day.
- Make or buy a paper cut-out of your theme's character for each child in class. Boldly print each child's name on the cut-out and display them on a special bulletin board in the classroom.
- Make or buy thematic nameplates for each student's desk.
- Use thematic bulletin board trimmer on your class bulletin boards. (If you have left-over trimmer, make a few thematic crowns for the student of the week to wear on his or her special day!)
- Use thematic clip art to make a variety of different awards, name tags, hall passes, notes home to parents, spelling list sheets, progress reports, etc.

You might want to select a thematic color for your awards, passes, etc., in addition to your theme. You might try lime green for *frogs*, turquoise blue for *dolphins*, hot pink for *ice cream*, goldenrod for *bears and bees*, bright yellow for *sun and stars* and bright red for *apples* and *lady bugs*.

On the following pages you will find generic forms and reports that you can personalize with your own thematic drawings or clip art. Simply reproduce them on colored paper to use during back to school or all year long!

STUDENT PASS TO THE

_____

This student has permission to

_____

_____

_____

_____
Teacher   Date

_____
Name

Did a Great Job Today!

_____
Teacher   Date

PROGRESS REPORT

_____
Student's Name

WEEK OF: _____

Reading: _____

Math: _____

Social Studies: _____

Science: _____

Behavior: _____

Teacher _____

Parent's Signature _____

(Please sign and return.)

Congratulations!

_____
Name

You have been recognized for...

_____

_____

_____

_____

_____

_____
Teacher   Date

Weekly Homework Assignments!

_____
Student's Name

Week of: _____

Monday _____

_____

Tuesday _____

_____

Wednesday _____

_____

Thursday _____

_____

Friday _____

_____

A Note to the Parent of:

_____

Student's Name

_____

Date

Dear Parent,

_____

_____

_____

_____

_____

_____

(Please respond at the bottom of this form and   _____
return it to me with your signature.)   Teacher

- -

                                     _____

                                       _____

_____

_____

_____

_____   _____

Date   Parent's Name

_____   _____

Student's Name   Parent's Signature

Classroom News!

Teacher_____ **Room #**_____

Date_____

Look What's Happening!

_____

_____

_____

_____

_____

Special Students!
_____
_____
_____

Upcoming Events!

_____

_____

_____

Help from Parents!

_____

_____

_____

How to Contact the Teacher!
_____
_____
_____

Classroom Signs!

TF0700 July & August Idea Book

121

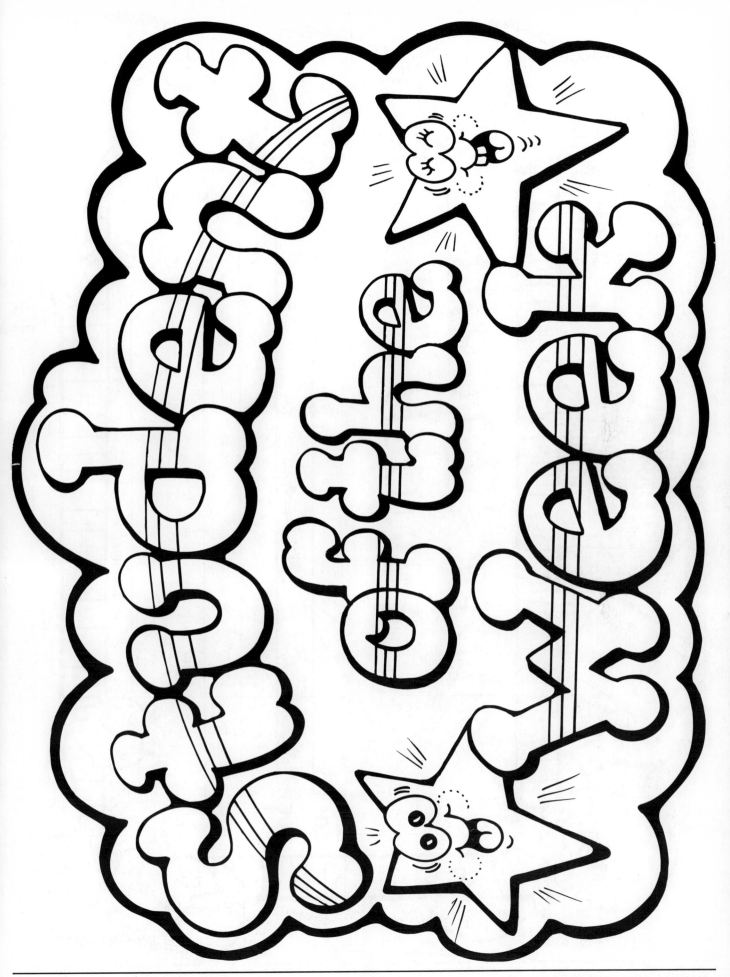

TF0700 July & August Idea Book

Super Student Award!

to:

for:

Teacher

Date

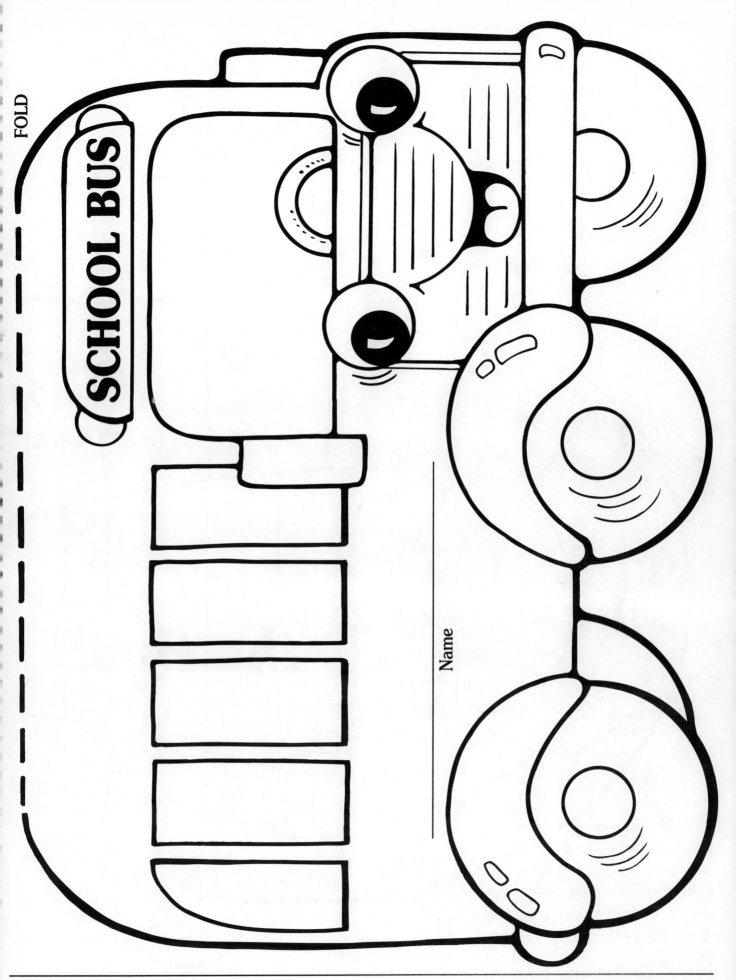

SCHOOL BUS

Name

1.

2.

3.

21.

20.

19.

18.

17.

22.

23.

24.

"Don't Miss
the Bus!"

25.

26.

27.

28.

29.

TEACHERS:
Two, three or
four children can
play this game. Make
your own task card or write
math problems, that must be
solved, in each square. The player
who reaches the school first wins
the game.

"Help these kids get to school!"

SCHOOL BUS RULES

1. The bus driver is the person in charge. You must do what he or she tells you to do.

2. Remain seated throughout the entire trip.

3. Keep all parts of your body inside the bus.

4. Do not throw anything inside the bus or out the windows..

5. Do not yell, scream, push, hit or kick while on the bus.

6. Sack lunches are allowed, but no food or drink may be eaten on the bus.

7. Do not keep another student from getting a seat.

8. Get off the bus at your correct bus stop.

9. When the driver has the flashing red lights on, cross the street with the driver.

10. Line up courteously at both your bus stop and the school.

I♥SKOOL

Name Mobiles

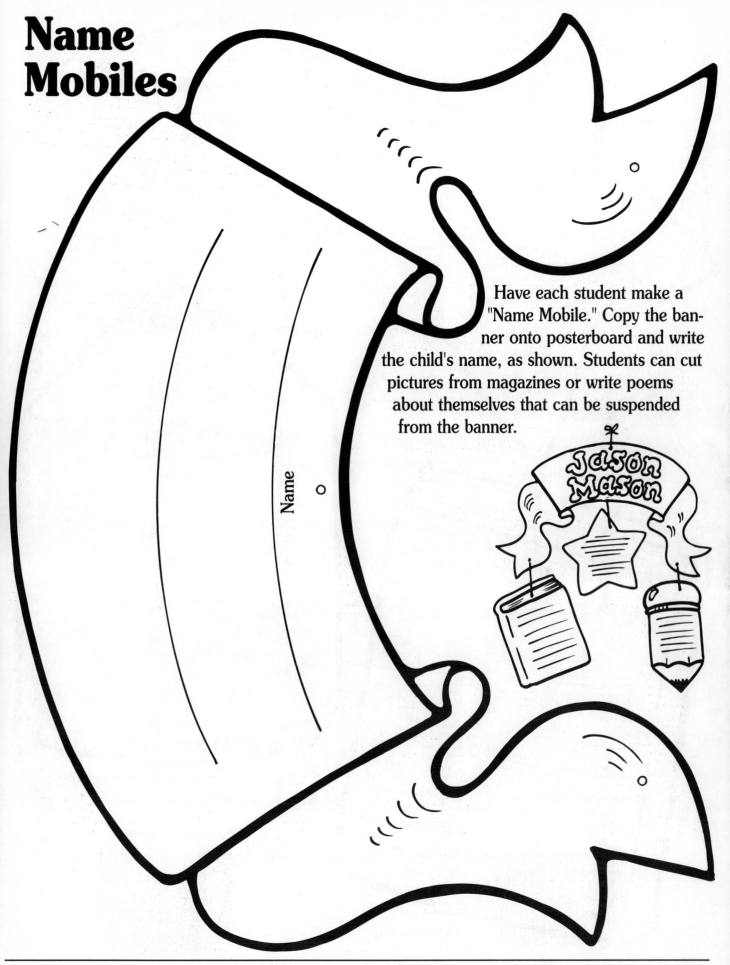

Have each student make a "Name Mobile." Copy the banner onto posterboard and write the child's name, as shown. Students can cut pictures from magazines or write poems about themselves that can be suspended from the banner.

Name

TF0700 July & August Idea Book

Name Mobile Patterns

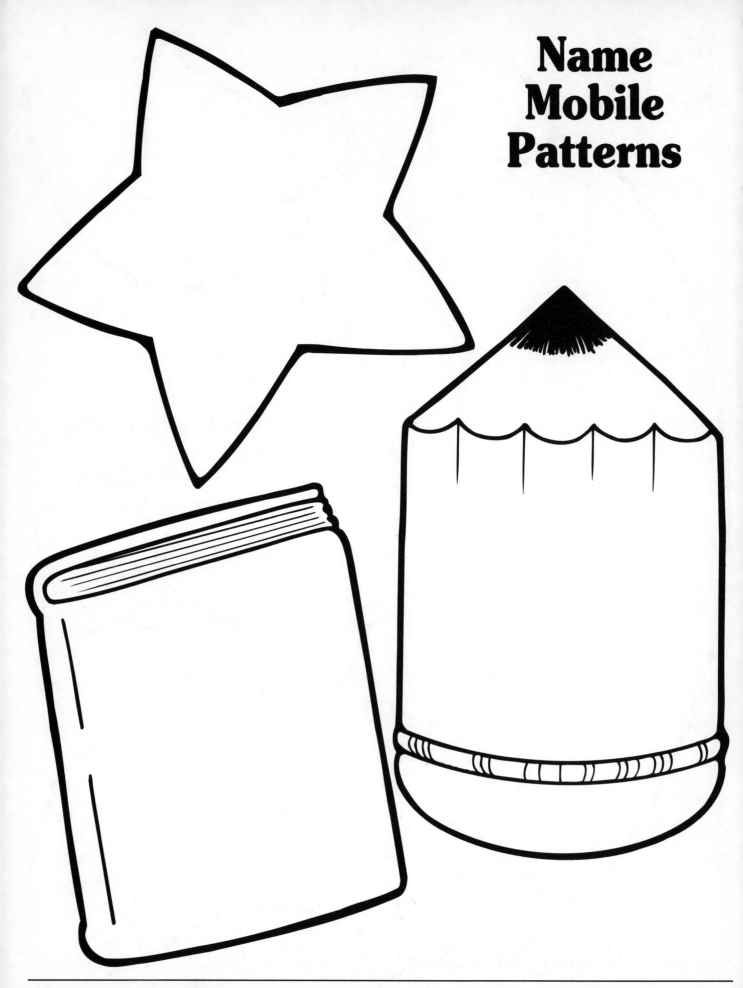

TF0700 July & August Idea Book

Bulletin Boards and More!

SHOOTING STARS!

Make everyone in class a super star with this idea. Each child can earn his or her own star and place it on the board when a particular task is accomplished. This is a great way to show off good work papers.

REACH FOR THE STARS!

Ask each child to write a goal on a yellow paper star. Pin the stars to the top of the bulletin board. Paper streamers can be added to each star. Next, have the students trace their right hands on colored construction paper. They should then add their names and pin each hand to the board under their chosen goal.

As goals are accomplished, small gold stars can be placed on the hands.

A GREAT BUNCH!

Cut large circles from purple construction paper for this simple board. Arrange them as shown and write each student's name on a grape. Children love to see their name in print and this bulletin board is a perfect way to do just that!

             TF0700 July & August Idea Book

Bulletin Boards and More!

SCHOOL BUS RULES

Display a large yellow school bus on the class bulletin board. List different rules of bus safety on strips of paper and arrange them around the bus. Children might like to draw portraits of themselves that can be placed in the bus windows.

SUMMERTIME HAPPENINGS

Display a large yellow sun in the center of the class bulletin board. Give each student a white paper cloud and ask them to write about their favorite summertime experience. Arrange the clouds around the sun for a bright and cheery display.

BLAST OFF TO LEARNING!

Cover your bulletin board with black butcher paper and string small, white, low-wattage Christmas lights around the border. Cut the title "Blast Off!" from silver foil and a star for each child from gold foil paper. Add a paper rocket ship.

Students' good work papers can be added to the display. Or, simply use this idea to welcome students to your class. On a large board, let children add their own imaginative creations such as planets, flying saucers or meteors.

133

Bulletin Boards and More!

KICK UP YOUR HEELS!

Give your students a "kick in the pants" with this motivating bulletin board idea!

Display a large cartoon horse on the board and give each student their own paper horseshoe. Have each pupil write his or her name on the horseshoe and pin it to the board. As they complete projects or improve behavior reward them with small gold

stars that can be placed on the horseshoes. Other possible titles of the board can be, "*We Don't Horse Around!*" or "*Giddy Up!*"

WE FIT IN!

Give each student a puzzle piece cut from brightly colored paper. (Pattern found in this chapter.) Assemble the puzzle pieces together on the class board to create a giant "We Fit In!" bulletin board!

GET GOING! BE SAFE!

Teach your students to be safe this summer by reinforcing the rules they should follow when crossing the street, riding a bike, riding in a car, etc. Use a cute traffic light pattern on the class board to remind students of the rules. Display the poem, "Red says *stop*! Green says *go*! Yellow says *wait*! You need to go *slow*!

Bulletin Boards and More!

CHOOSE WELL

Encourage your students to wisely choose the types of foods they eat with this simple bulletin board. The students can cut food pictures from magazines or draw their own nutritious goodies.

TELEPHONE NUMBERS

Teach your students important numbers along with their home phone numbers with this simple bulletin board. As each child memorizes their phone number, they can write it on a strip of paper along with their name and display it on the board around a large paper telephone. Also, encourage them to memorize emergency numbers.

WE'RE REALLY COOKING!

Let your students display creative recipes with this easy bulletin board. Cut a large French chef from colored paper and place him or her on one side of the board. Students can write their recipes on recipe cards and display them around the chef.

Shoe Pattern

Students will love to learn to tie their shoes with this easy craft.

Copy the pattern of this shoe onto posterboard. Punch out the holes with a hole punch. Cut a length of yarn about 28 inches long and wrap tape around the ends to prevent fraying. When students demonstrate their ability to tie their shoes, give them this shoe to tie and display it on the class bulletin board.

Label the bulletin board "Our class really steps to it!" or "We're right in step!"

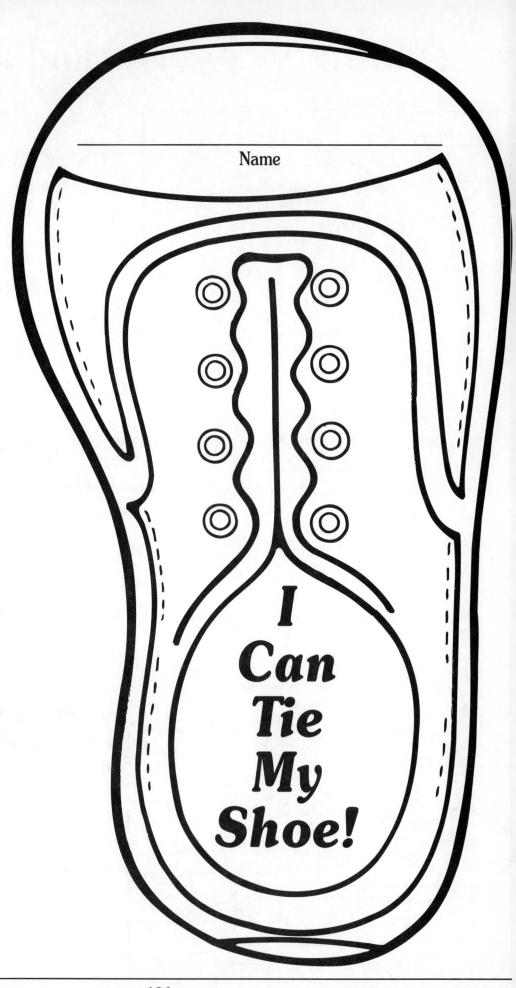

Name

I Can Tie My Shoe!

Phone Pattern

I know
my phone
number!

I know my phone
number!

_____

Name

_____

Phone Number

 TF0700 July & August Idea Book

Name

Cut two of each pattern piece. Glue the patterns back-to-back with a string down the center to make the mobile.

Hamburger Mobile!

Student Puzzle Pieces!

Have students cut their own puzzle pieces from heavy colored paper. Use a variety of colors if possible. Students can fill in their own information. Assemble the puzzle pieces together on the class board to create one giant classroom puzzle!

My Name: _____

_____

My Favorites!

Color:

_____

Food:

_____

Hobby:

_____

School Subjects:

_____

_____

A Picture of Me!

I'm Special!

Welcome
Bear
Pattern

WELCOME!

TF0700 July & August Idea Book

Answer Key!

Patriotic Fun!

ACTIVITY 1

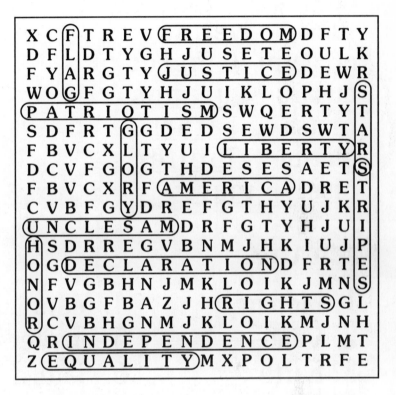

```
X C F T R E V F R E E D O M D F T Y
D F L D T Y G H J U S E T E O U L K
F Y A R G T Y J U S T I C E D E W R
W O G F G T Y H J U I K L O P H J S
P A T R I O T I S M S W Q E R T Y T
S D F R T G G D E D S E W D S W T A
F B V C X L T Y U I L I B E R T Y R
D C V F G O G T H D E S E S A E T S
F B V C X R F A M E R I C A D R E T
C V B F G Y D R E F G T H Y U J K R
U N C L E S A M D R F G T Y H J U I
H S D R R E G V B N M J H K I U J P
O G D E C L A R A T I O N D F R T E
N F V G B H N J M K L O I K J M N S
O V B G F B A Z J H R I G H T S G L
R C V B H G N M J K L O I K M J N H
Q R I N D E P E N D E N C E P L M T
Z E Q U A L I T Y M X P O L T R F E
```

ACTIVITY 2

THE STATUE OF LIBERTY

Answer Key!
Space Fun!

ACTIVITY 3

htaer   <u>earth</u>
toupl   <u>pluto</u>
neutpne   <u>neptune</u>
suevn   <u>venus</u>
urcyerm   <u>mercury</u>
nusaru   <u>uranus</u>
rnutsa   <u>saturn</u>
piertuj   <u>jupiter</u>
rasm   <u>mars</u>

ACTIVITY 4

1. Mercury
2. Venus
3. Earth
4. Mars
5. Jupiter
6. Saturn
7. Uranus
8. Neptune
9. Pluto

ACTIVITY 5

```
S W E R D S H U T T L E D R E W Q G H Y T
D O D C V F G T R E W S C B G Y T U I P O
S R H Y A S T R O N A U T D E R C Y T H U
C B Y H U J I Y N M H Y T R F R O D R E T
D I S A T E L L I T E D R E R F M G T Y U
S T E L E S C O P E F R V S G T E U I P L
A S D F C V B G T R E D A T D E T F E W S
M E T E O R D R E F R G E A F E W Z X V B
O D E R F H T R W F G B H R R D W C V G H
O D R E A S T E R O I D F V B G H Y T N M
N F R E S D G B F T R E W Q A D F R T G H
K L P L A N E T S T G H Y U N M J K I U H
D C V G F T Y H J A S T R O N O M Y V C X
```

TF0700 July & August Idea Book

Thematic Index to Teacher's Friend Monthly Books!

TF0100 January Idea Book
TF0200 February Idea Book
TF0300 March Idea Book
TF0400 April Idea Book
TF0500 May Idea Book
TF0600 June Idea Book

TF0700 July & Aug. Idea Book
TF0900 September Idea Book
TF1000 October Idea Book
TF1100 November Idea Book
TF1200 December Idea Book

Find these and all Teacher's Friend products at your local Educational Supply Store!

A

African-American Achievers
February Idea Book
Alligators
June Idea Book
American Indians
September Idea Book
November Idea Book
Amphibians
June Idea Book
Apples
September Idea Book
April Fool's Day
April Idea Book
Arbor Day
April Idea Book
Arctic and Antarctic Animals
January Idea Book
Autumn
September Idea Book
October Idea Book
November Idea Book

B

Back to School
September Idea Book
July & Aug. Idea Book
Bears
September Idea Book
November Idea Book
July & Aug. Idea Book
January Idea Book
July & Aug. Idea Book
Bees
April Idea Book
Birds
May Idea Book
Birthdays
September Idea Book
Black History
January Idea Book
February Idea Book
March Idea Book
Bugs (Insects)
April Idea Book
Butterflies
April Idea Book

C

Calendars
(Each book has a monthly calendar)
January Idea Book
Cats
February Idea Book
Chicken and Egg
April Idea Book
Children's Book Week
November Idea Book
Chinese New Year
January Idea Book
Christmas
December Idea Book
Christmas (International)
Mexico, Italy, Holland, Sweden
December Idea Book
Cinco De Mayo
May Idea Book
Clowns and Circus
May Idea Book
September Idea Book
Colors
March Idea Book
Columbus Day
October Idea Book
Cowboys/Cowgirls
July & Aug. Idea Book

D

Dental Health
February Idea Book
Dinosaurs
October Idea Book
Dogs
February Idea Book

E

Earth Day
April Idea Book
Easter
April Idea Book
Election Day
November Idea Book
End of the School Year
June Idea Book

Environmental Awareness
April Idea Book
Eskimos
January Idea Book

F

Farm Animals
March Idea Book
Father's Day
June Idea Book
Field Trips
May Idea Book
Fire Safety
October Idea Book
Fish
June Idea Book
Flag Day
June Idea Book
Flowers
April Idea Book
May Idea Book
Frogs
June Idea Book
March Idea Book
Fourth of July
July & Aug. Idea Book

G

Gingerbread Man
December Idea Book
Grandparent's Day
September Idea Book
Groundhog Day
February Idea Book
Growing Things
May Idea Book
November Idea Book

H

Halloween
October Idea Book
Hanukkah
Harvest Time
November Idea Book
May Idea Book
Heart Health
February Idea Book
Horses
July & Aug. Idea Book

Thematic Index to Teacher's Friend Monthly Books!

I

Ice Cream
July & Aug. Idea Book
Insects
April Idea Book
International Children
Africa
December Idea Book
China
January Idea Book
Eskimos
January Idea Book
Greece
April Idea Book
Holland
December Idea Book
Ireland
March Idea Book
Israel
December Idea Book
Italy
December Idea Book
Japan
March Idea Book
Mexico
December Idea Book
Native North American
September Idea Book
Pacific Islands
June Idea Book
Pilgrims
November Idea Book
Russia
May Idea Book
Sweden
December Idea Book
United States
School Kids
September Idea Book
Summer Kids
June Idea Book

J

Japan
March Idea Book

K

King, Jr., Martin Luther
January Idea Book
Kwanzaa
December Idea Book

L

Leaves/Trees
October Idea Book
April Idea Book
Leprechauns
March Idea Book
Library Activities
November Idea Book
Lincoln, Abraham
February Idea Book

M

Masks
October Idea Book
May Day
May Idea Book
Mexican Independence Day
September Idea Book
Mexico
September Idea Book
December Idea Book
May Idea Book
Mother's Day
May Idea Book
Music Appreciation
March Idea Book
My "Me" Book!
September Idea Book

N

Names
September Idea Book
July & Aug. Idea Book
New Year's Day
January Idea Book
Nutrition
July & Aug. Idea Book

O

Oceanography
June Idea Book
Olympics
April Idea Book
Owls
September Idea Book
October Idea Book

P

Parent-Teacher Conferences
November Idea Book
Pilgrims
November Idea Book
Pirates
June Idea Book
Pizza
July & Aug. Idea Book
December Idea Book
Pledge of Allegiance
June Idea Book
Presidents
February Idea Book
November Idea Book
Promotion
June Idea Book

R

Rabbits
April Idea Book
Rainbows
March Idea Book
Reptiles
June Idea Book

S

School Bus
July & Aug. Idea Book
Seashore
June Idea Book
Seasons
January Idea Book
September Idea Book
Skeleton
October Idea Book
Snakes
June Idea Book
Solar System
July & Aug. Idea Book

South Pacific
June Idea Book
Space/Universe
July & Aug. Idea Book
Spiders
October Idea Book
Springtime
March Idea Book
April Idea Book
May Idea Book
States and Capitals
November Idea Book
St. Patrick's Day
March Idea Book
Student Teachers
September Idea Book
Substitute Teachers
September Idea Book
Summer
June Idea Book
July & Aug. Idea Book
Sun/Sunshine
July & Aug. Idea Book

T
Teeth
February Idea Book
Thanksgiving
November Idea Book
Turkeys
November Idea Book
Turtles
June Idea Book

U
Umbrellas
April Idea Book

V
Valentine's Day
February Idea Book

W
Washington, George
February Idea Book
Watermelons
July & Aug. Idea Book
Weather
March Idea Book
April Idea Book
Whales
June Idea Book
Wild West
July & Aug. Idea Book
Winter
December Idea Book
January Idea Book
February Idea Book
Women in History
March Idea Book
Woodsy Animals
November Idea Book

Y
Year-Round
September Idea Book
January Idea Book

Z
Zoo Animals
May Idea Book